796.352 Gol

Golf tips from the pros.

PRICE: $11.99 (an/dar)

GOLF TIPS
FROM THE PROS

A DAVID & CHARLES BOOK

Copyright © David & Charles Limited 2006

David & Charles is an F+W Publications Inc. company
4700 East Galbraith Road, Cincinnati, OH 45236

First published in the UK in 2006

Source material courtesy of *Golf World* magazine copyright © Emap Active
Photography by Bob Atkins, James Cheadle, Getty Images and Angus Murray

A catalogue record for this book is available from the British Library.

ISBN-13: 978-0-7153-2257-4
ISBN-10: 0-7153-2257-5

Printed in China by SNP Leefung
for David & Charles
Brunel House   Newton Abbot   Devon

Visit our website at www.davidandcharles.co.uk

David & Charles books are available from all good bookshops;
alternatively you can contact our Orderline on 0870 9908222
or write to us at FREEPOST EX2 110, D&C Direct, Newton Abbot,
TQ12 4ZZ (no stamp required UK only); US customers call
800-289-0963 and Canadian customers call 800-840-5220.

GOLF TIPS
FROM THE PROS

Edited by Tim Baker

David and Charles

Contents

↑ ↑ ↑

Bunker Play 76

Short Game 92

Trouble Spots 122

Putting 142

Practice 166

Contents

↑ ↑ ↑ ↑

→ → → Introduction

It is the nature of the game of golf that we are all searching for that magic formula, that tweak in technique that is going to turn us from chumps to champs and lead to glorious rounds of perfect striking and putts dropping with the sun on our backs and the birds singing. And it is not just the amateurs and high-handicap hackers that spend their golfing life striving for this – far from being the perfect golfing machines we imagine they are, the world's top players are always worrying about and tinkering with their technique, discovering new swing thoughts and passing each other tips on new putting grips, alignment methods or practice routines.

Of course the pros know that one magic tip cannot revolutionize their game, just as the struggling amateur will know from experience that no quick fix can make up for a faulty technique. Any good player will tell you that you must start with the fundamentals of good technique and practise, practise, practise. Many of the invaluable tips in this book address those very fundamentals that are every bit as important to the touring pros as they should be to the improving high-handicapper. But as well as sound technique you will find a host of golfing tips that give a fascinating insight into what goes through the minds of the world's great players as they compile their bogey-free rounds. There's no substitute for hearing it from the horse's mouth and the tips you will learn from this book are all the proven techniques of international winners. Somewhere here may be 'the answer', or on the other hand you may struggle to make a tip work for you, but if it works for Seve or Nick or Ernie or Tiger or Vijay, it's probably worth a try.

→ → → The Golf Swing

What could be easier than swinging a golf club? Surely it's merely a question of swishing it over your shoulder and then sweeping it back down again to send the ball soaring majestically towards its target? If only things were that straight-forward – we'd all then be shooting sub-par rounds at our local course and jostling with Tiger Woods to win the next Major. A good swing may look simple, but the time spent by professionals tweaking and remodelling their swing, together with the host of coaches eager to offer advice, are eloquent testimony to the pitfalls in this most basic aspect of the game. Its importance cannot be overstated. Though a few mavericks make it to the very top despite having highly unorthodox swings, most players are doomed to perennial struggle if the key ingredients of a good swing are lacking. This chapter shows what those ingredients are, and how to integrate them into your game.

How to obtain the perfect grip

Amateurs are inclined to ignore fundamentals such as the grip. I've seen eyes glaze over when I try to pass on a tip or two about this part of the game. That may be your impression now. But don't turn over! It may be a cliché but your hands are the only contact with the club. It pays to do it right. Here are two good reasons why.

First, a good grip helps you generate more power, because if the grip is neutral it's more likely the clubface stays neutral throughout the swing and you can release it freely with the face returning to square at impact.

If your grip is too strong, where your hands are turned over too far to the right, releasing the club shuts the clubface and you hit the ball miles left. So to avoid that you have to hold-off the clubface through the ball, which kills speed. A strong grip by name, then, but weak by nature.

Also if you've got a good grip the left thumb can support the club at the top of your backswing, as you can see in the picture opposite,

so you get a much more solid and compact position.

If your grip is too strong, your thumb is in no position to support the club at the top and during the downswing. As a result your ball striking is bound to suffer.

Take hold of the club with your left hand. You should be able to see at least two-and-a-half knuckles.

The Golf Swing

↑ ↑ ↑ ↑

Now add your right hand to the grip, with the V formed by thumb and forefinger pointing at your right shoulder.

Don't forget that a soft hold works best

Tension in the hands at address causes 'gridlock' in the arms and shoulders, which restricts movement. Remember to keep your hold on the club nice and soft, so that your hands and arms feel relaxed as you address the ball, primed to generate maximum clubhead speed.

The thumb of your left hand should support the club as it nears the top of the backswing.

Set up for swing success

My swing fundamentals all derive from a good set-up. I try to get great weight distribution, maybe just a little bit more on my right side than my left, say 60 per cent to 40 per cent. I do this to avoid too much tilt in my shoulders – the more tilt you have, the more the club will get stuck inside and will come straight inside, forcing you to work it over the top.

What I try to do is set up in a position that requires very little compensation or re-routing to be made. When you look at Jim Furyk, who has his hands really close to his body at address, he has to take the club out away from his body and re-route it back in to clear his hips. All this is caused by him needing to compensate for his set-up position. When I am playing really well I feel that I am set up properly. I don't have too much sideways action on my ball and hit it pretty much where I am aiming. That is where ideally your set-up should be.

The shoulders should be slightly tilted, with the head just behind the ball.

Too much tilt in your shoulders will lead to the club getting stuck inside and force you to work it over the top.

Maintain the triangle and make a full shoulder turn.

Set up with your club as an extension of your arms so that little re-routing is needed.

1 Slightly flex your right leg so that your weight favours the right side. From there, the arms and shoulders form a triangle.

2 Avoid going too fast with either the upper or lower body and letting them take over. Stretching the arms away from the ball ensures that the club is swung on the correct path.

→ Paul Casey

Stand the right distance from the ball

When I was playing in the Dunhill Links Championship recently, I was really struggling with my game and I realized it was because I was wearing a lot of layers, including waterproofs, which were causing me to stand too far from the ball. So I devised an easy way of checking my set-up position and how far away I should stand.

Set-up

Set up to a perfect postion on the practice range. Get a better player or ideally the club pro to help you with this. Then lay a 6-iron along your toes and a 5-iron at a right angle to this. Mark the shaft of the 6-iron where your toes touch it and opposite the ideal ball position agreed for a 7-iron.

Ball position

The shaft pointing at a right angle away from you should then be marked where the ideal ball position is for a 7-iron shot. Other marks can be made to show the ideal position for other clubs, too. Mark the shaft at one-inch intervals going away from you. Each inch signifies one longer club. Then make marks at one-inch intervals coming back towards you – for each club less than a 7-iron.

Drills

Then, whenever you practise, lay these down and make sure your feet and the ball position are lined up with the marks on the shaft along your toes. Also ensure the club is positioned behind the ball, level with the mark on the horizontal shaft. That way you will know you are always practising in the correct set-up position. This will promote a good set-up and stance on the course.

The Golf Swing

↑ ↑ ↑ ↑

Bernard Gallacher

Work on the basics

I'm a great believer in paying most attention to the basics. I work on my alignment, posture, also on making sure my grip is always correct. I would say if I were giving someone a lesson, 80 per cent of my advice would relate to these basics such as alignment, grip and posture. Many club golfers don't realise that slight faults at address trigger serious faults in the swing. All the great players seem to me to always be checking the simple things.

As for swing thoughts, I keep them pretty simple too. A niggling fault of mine is to get the clubface a little shut in the backswing, so when I'm playing a practice round I work on rotating my left arm in the backswing so that the clubface is distinctly open at the top. This means I sometimes have a tendency to leave the occasional iron shot out to the right, but that wouldn't happen in a competition. The extra adrenaline that comes with playing in a tournament would get me squaring the face a little sooner in the downswing and I'd hit them straight.

I also like to feel that I point the club at the target at the top of my backswing. Then, as I start down, I turn my body out of the way and swing the club into the space I've created, keep turning my left side out of the way, and release the club to the inside going through.

Build a model backswing

I firmly believe that any golfer can achieve a certain amount of success by concentrating on developing a better backswing. If it's not properly performed, then you can't expect much from the downswing. Remember, a good swing is fluent from the start to the finish.

1 Initiate the backswing by synchronizing the movement of the club, head, hands, arms and body.

2 When the clubhead points to 8 o'clock, the butt end of the club should point to the middle of your right thigh.

3 Practise resting the butt end of the club in your navel and turn your stomach and club away together.

Butt drill
Make sure the butt doesn't become separated as you turn away.

The Golf Swing

↑ ↑ ↑

→ Jay Haas
Keep your height for solid contact

One of my aims over the past year or so has been to try and stay level in my swing – from address, through my backswing and all the way into the hitting area.

Swing path
If I can stay level, my swing path is a little more level, or shallow, coming into the ball and I seem to take less of a divot. And I usually hit it a little more solidly that way.

Head
I try to keep my head up so that I don't dip down as I come into the ball.

Balance
Hitting too hard is a common mistake at club level. It causes you to lose your co-ordination and your balance. Basically, the shape of your swing is ruined. Swing easy.

Knees
The mistake I make when I try to hit the ball hard is to squat into the ball and lose my height. Keeping your knees level as you swing means you're more likely to maintain the proper angles. As a result, you'll make more consistent contact.

Chin up

Forget the old saying about keeping your head down. That's rubbish! It just gets in the way of a good shoulder turn. Instead, think of keeping your chin up to give yourself space into which to turn your left shoulder at the top of the backswing.

Waggling the golf club will help you prepare for the shot.

Keep your chin up throughout the swing.

The Golf Swing

↑ ↑ ↑

18

Stay focused
on the ball on
the down-
swing.

It's important
to clear the left
side through
impact. Your
head turns with
your body.

Face the target
at the end of the
swing.

Stay level in the swing

In any sport you'll always have people who make it to the top despite playing with an unconventional technique. Golf is no exception. But by and large the more things you do correctly in the swing, the easier it is to play consistently to a decent standard. One of the best things to work on is keeping your head level in the swing and making sure you do not lose or gain height.

If you want a classic role model in this department, look at someone like Ernie Els. His head stays nice and level throughout the swing, until the ball is well on its way. It's something I've worked hard to get right in my own swing.

The Golf Swing

↑ ↑ ↑

Try to feel that your head stays level throughout your backswing. Hovering the clubhead prevents jerks.

Keep things smooth as you start the downswing.

If you keep your head level in the swing, it means the club is more likely to return to the point where it started at address, so you get better consistency of strike. It also means you can swing the club freely down and through impact without the need to make any last split-second adjustments. So you get more clubhead speed.

That isn't the case if you let your head bob up and down. The fault I see most often among amateurs is the head going down in the backswing and then coming up again in the downswing. That costs so much in terms of ball striking. Not only are compensations needed in order to find the middle of the clubface, but your weight isn't moving into the back of the ball to support the strike. So keep this in mind. As you make a practice swing, try to feel that your head stays level throughout your backswing and towards impact. Even better, rehearse it in front of a mirror or a large window.

Notice how the head stays level as the club comes down and into impact.

It's only after impact that the head starts to move.

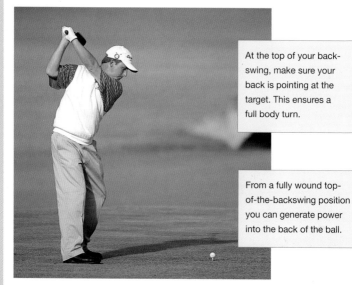

➡ **David Toms**
Turn for power

Henry Cotton once said that 'completing a full body pivot is seen in the play of all good golfers. Some achieve this with the left heel planted on the ground, others need an easing of the left heel off the ground. It all depends on the level of flexibility of the player.'

That statement has as much relevance today as it did nearly 50 years ago and is shown by the picture below of David Toms putting Cotton's words into practice. Toms has an elegant, rhythmical swing, with very little wasted energy – he hits the ball a long way through getting the fundamentals right, rather than out-and-out power. In that sense he's in a similar mould to the likes of, say, Davis Love III.

Toms is very flexible because he is able to make a big turn without the need to lift his left heel even a fraction off the ground. But whether you keep your left heel grounded or not is unimportant. What's far more relevant is that you are able to emulate Toms and complete a full shoulder turn at the top of the backswing.

At the top of your backswing, make sure your back is pointing at the target. This ensures a full body turn.

From a fully wound top-of-the-backswing position you can generate power into the back of the ball.

The Golf Swing

↑ ↑ ↑ ↑

→ Ernie Els
Align your shoulders

High on the list of most common faults among golfers is poor alignment, especially with the shoulders. And it's nearly always because players aim left. Even the greats, such as Ernie Els, can drift into this bad habit if left unchecked for any length of time. The trouble is, if the shoulders are out of line then so usually is the swing path. So keep a regular check on this aspect of your set-up. Have a friend check it, or video yourself, to make sure your shoulder line is parallel with the target line.

1 If you've been aligned too far left, you'll feel as if you're looking almost over your shoulder. Instead, from a confirmed correct position get used to the 'view' over your left shoulder in your peripheral vision. Stick to that. Use it as a reference point, a swing thought if you like, when you're on the golf course.

2 One additional benefit of your shoulders being aligned correctly is that you don't have as far to turn them to get to the required 90 degrees at the top of your backswing. If your shoulders are 20 degrees open, your shoulders have to travel 110 degrees to arrive at an orthodox position. That's asking an awful lot.

3 (Right) Your toe-line at address should correspond with your shoulder line.

➡ **Retief Goosen**

Point your club at the target

Retief Goosen hasn't got a coach, but that doesn't stop this gifted player finding some textbook positions in the swing. None are any better than that illustrated below. No wonder Retief hitting long irons is one of the finest sights in golf.

This photo also brings to mind a favourite gem of advice from the legendary teacher John Jacobs. Given a pupil who doesn't set the club correctly at the top of the swing, with perhaps too much body motion and not enough arm swing, John says: 'Try to feel that you point the club at the target at the top of the swing.' Just as Retief does here.

With that objective in mind, the arm swing starts to work more in harmony with the body motion and the result is a hugely improved top-of-the-backswing position. Try it. You'll be amazed how effective this simplest of swing thoughts can be.

1 Goosen's club is pointing directly at the target at the top of his backswing. Try to hold that thought during the swing – it will help prevent overswinging, which usually leads to a poorly struck shot.

2 Feel your left shoulder under your chin. This ensures a full upper body turn, making the arms and hands less active.

3 The right knee stays flexed throughout, allowing the upper body to turn but not permitting too much rotation.

⬆ ⬆ ⬆

→ Ian Poulter

Shake hands with the target

Any golfer who slices the ball is failing to release the club properly through the hitting area. That's an indisputable fact. And as any sufferer knows, it costs you distance as the ball leaks frustratingly to the right on pretty much every long shot you hit. This picture of Ian Poulter represents a simple, graphic image to help cure that problem.

Basically, you need to think in terms of trying to shake hands with the target as you swing through impact. By doing that, you'll generate a much freer release of the clubhead, which increases your speed through the ball, enabling you to hit it further. Also, you'll have less of a tendency to meet the ball with an open clubface. With practice, your slice is slowly eradicated.

Visualize this image as you make practice swings, then try to replicate it in your actual swing.

1 Pleased to meet you: visualizing shaking hands with the target ensures your hands get through the ball, releasing the clubhead and eliminating the dreaded slice.

2 Notice how Poulter has completed a full shoulder turn and extended his arms through the hitting area and out towards the target. A classic follow-through.

Maintain the triangle for better striking

I've always had a tendency to get a little 'handsy' at the start of my swing, picking the club up a little too steeply and not in tune with my body action, which I know is something a lot of club golfers do as well. It's one of the major reasons a lot of golfers slice, because it sets the club outside the line at the start of the swing and it's tough to recover that.

So, what I'm trying to do to prevent that happening is concentrate on maintaining the triangle in my forearms for longer into my take-away. It gives me more width in my swing and also keeps the club going back on the correct path.

That first part of the swing is so important. If your hands play such an active role in the takeaway, it's inevitable that the club is going to go back on an incorrect path, which means you have to make compensations later in the swing. So save yourself that problem and focus on the first move away from the ball. Keep that triangle intact by feeling that you take the club back with your arms and shoulders, rather than your hands. It will help the club stay more on line and your whole swing benefits as a result.

Here the triangle has broken down, with the club being taken away too much on the inside.

Here the club is going back outside the correct plane. Again the triangle has broken down.

The Golf Swing

⬆️ ⬆️ ⬆️

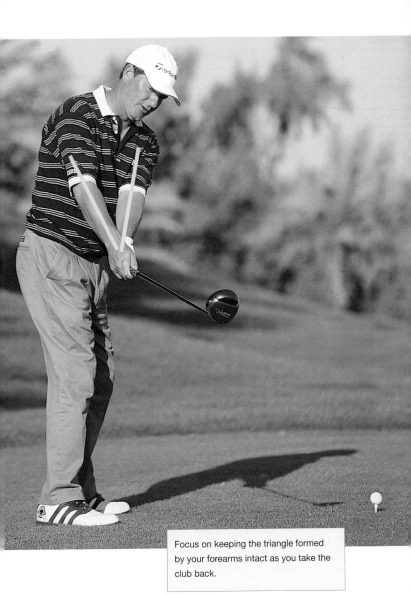

Focus on keeping the triangle formed by your forearms intact as you take the club back.

Improve your ball striking

It's been said that the top of the backswing can make or break any shot you might be taking on. So this is an area of the swing I've paid a lot of attention to because it really is that important.

A good drill to give you a feeling for starting the downswing is to adopt good posture without a club in your hands. Your arms should hang down with your palms facing in. In slow motion make a swing where your hands and arms work in harmony with your body, swinging in front of the body. The one single key to focus on during the downswing is to make sure the hands stay in front of your body

Posture
The hands hang down, palms facing in.

The Golf Swing

↑ ↑ ↑

as you swing back and down. That helps me 'time' the swinging arms with the turning motion of the body. Then complete the follow-through.

Now grab a golf club and make slow motion swings, again trying to focus on the same feeling of everything moving together. It takes some perfecting, but the intention alone should be enough to see an improvement, and with regular practice of this drill, you should find yourself striking the ball much more clearly.

Swing
Keep the hands swinging in front of the body.

Finish
Make sure you complete the follow-through.

How to play a draw

Starting with target line and body parallel, as if following the lines on a railway track, to hit the draw I simply keep the ball and club-head pointing along the outside track and then aim my feet, knees, hips, shoulders and forearms to the right of the inside track. I then swing along the line of my body, which means that I am now coming 'around' the ball with the swing coming from the inside. And because the face is now closed to the line I am swinging on, it should produce a consistent and smooth draw spin on the ball.

The backswing

Keep the club tracking slightly on an inside path as the hands and arms take away.

At the top

The hands are lower at the top, encouraging a flatter, more rounded swing plane.

At impact

The body stays back, allowing the hands and arms to release through the hitting area.

The follow-through

Swing through to a balanced position facing the target and watch the ball draw.

The Golf Swing

↑ ↑ ↑ ↑

How to play a fade

To hit the fade shot I simply do the opposite of the draw shot. So, I keep the ball and clubhead pointing along the outside track and then aim my feet, knees, hips, shoulders and forearms to the left of the inside track. I then swing along the line of my body, which means that I attack the ball more from the outside, and because the face is now open to the line I am swinging on, it will produce cut spin on the ball.

The backswing
Keep the club tracking slightly on the outside as the hands and arms take away.

At the top
The clubface is wide open to the target line at the top of the backswing.

At impact
The hands should stay firm, resisting the release. Do not allow them to roll over.

The follow-through
This will be higher as a result of the out-to-in swing path, as the hands resist the release.

Control your downswing

Controlling what you do in the downswing is never easy, because everything is happening pretty fast, so the trick is this. Learn to co-ordinate the movement of your arm swing and body turn in your backswing and, as a result of that, your downswing will be better co-ordinated, too. The hands and arms have further to travel than the shoulders, so it makes sense they should get a head start. That's the specific 'feeling' you need. From halfway back, you should then think of the arms and body completing the backswing at the same time. These swing thoughts should help synchronize your arms and body and get you into a good slot at the top. From there, you've got a better chance of making a good downswing.

From halfway back, think about the arms and body completing the backswing at the same time.

Run your swing on autopilot

This tip is based on a Faldo video I watched as an amateur in the late 1980s. In the film, Faldo hit 10 shots in a row but you didn't see the club he was using. It was easy to assume he was hitting the same club, as his swing didn't change. In actual fact he hit five different clubs, from his wedge to his driver. His tempo and swing didn't change. That's a great piece of advice. We all try to help the ball into the air with our long irons and swing too fast with our driver, but our best shots come when we just swing the same with these clubs as we do with a wedge. The only difference is the length and the loft of the club. Ignore them both, for the ball doesn't recognize which club is hitting it! The difference you feel is all in the mind.

Imagination
Every club in the bag should be swung exactly the same. If you worry about hitting a 4-iron, simply imagine you have an 8-iron in your hands.

Timing and tempo
Next time you go to the driving range set your swing like a metronome and keep your timing and tempo exactly the same with every club.

→ → → Driving

Everyone who picks up a golf club in earnest has visions of hammering the ball off the tee and watching it disappear down the fairway into the distance. Without doubt that's one of the games most satisfying experiences, but it's one that most amateurs enjoy all too rarely. Such are the problems encountered in using a driver that some give up using it altogether, opting instead for the relative safety of an iron. Yet much of the difficulty is more imagined than real, most of it down to faulty technique that can swiftly be put right. This chapter gives tips on how to use the driver effectively and banish those first-tee fears. Learn the lessons given here and you will be a step closer to attaining the majestic drives you crave.

Hit away from trouble

Nine times out of ten I'd advise amateurs to take the safe option of playing an iron off the tee on tough holes like the one pictured right. But at the same time I understand that part of the fun of golf is giving your driver a good old-fashioned dig. Also, there are times when you might want to attack – in a matchplay situation, for instance. Or in a friendly game when there's no score to protect. If that's the case, here's how to attack in a smart way, saving you the need to resort to a crude hit-and-hope shot.

Aim where you want the ball to go

A greenkeeper won't deliberately set out to point the tee boxes in the wrong direction, but it might easily happen by accident and often does. It's dangerous because if you're not careful it can easily lead you to aim somewhere other than the middle of the fairway. It plays tricks with your vision. So make sure you aim where you want to go, not where the tee markers are pointing you. It takes only a second to check – by standing behind the ball and looking down the teeing ground – and could save you shots.

Driving

↑ ↑ ↑

1 The first step is to make full use of the teeing area. Don't tee the ball just anywhere. For the shot illustrated here, tee up on the right-hand side of the teeing ground, the side where the trouble is, and aim at the opposite side of the fairway.

2 If the ball starts in a safe direction, it's got to curve the entire width of the fairway to find trouble. If you aim down the centre, the ball has to move only half the width of the fairway to find trouble. That's a big difference – you increase your margin of error by 50 per cent.

3 Even if you hit a straight ball, this is a smart move. If you fade or slice, it's essential. So pick a distinguishing mark down the safe side of the fairway and make that your target. Try to focus on that spot and nothing else. Easier said than done, but possible.

➡️ **Bernhard Langer**

Beat the first-tee blues

Try to enjoy the moment, that's the first thing. Take a few deep breaths just before you set up to the ball; that always helps. And try to swing the club smoothly. Most amateurs swing way too hard anyway, and if you're nervous that usually just makes things worse.

Make sure you get to the tee in good time, as well. That's a simple thing, but it's important: rushing around won't do you any good. Find time to hit a few practice shots beforehand.

Remember that you don't have to prove anything to anyone, and that will help you relax a bit too. I often say this to pro-am partners if they're nervous on the first tee. I mean, we all know how difficult the game is so don't put extra pressure on yourself!

Driving

↑ ↑ ↑

The goalie stance

Try adopting an athletic posture without a club – like a goalie would stand.
This drill will help you get a feeling of a good posture position at address.

Hands should be forward to encourage a good body position.

Feel the weight on the balls of your feet – you could even lift your heels off the floor to exaggerate this feeling.

Bend forward from the hips, keeping your spine straight.

Hover your driver

I can't stand being stuck in a static position over the ball. It's a real killer, because it upsets the rhythm of the swing. That's why I like to stay 'fluid' at address. I don't ground the club and I make sure I waggle it a few times before I start my swing. You should do the same. It stops you getting stuck at address. From there you'll find you can flow into your backswing a lot more smoothly and the rhythm of your whole swing improves as a result.

Hover the club at address to promote a smooth first move.

Remember this

Don't ruin that smooth start by trying to hit the ball too hard. You should only ever swing your driver at a maximum 90 per cent power. Never go above that. If you do, chances are you're going to hit a seriously bad tee shot right there, which is damaging enough in itself. Worse still, you can upset your rhythm and that can be tough to get back.

Driving

Nick Dougherty
Tame your tempo

The most common mistake amateurs make is to try and kill their driver. This makes their swing quick and snatchy. By swinging slower it gives you more time to get your body and arm movement in harmony and you will generate more power.

Breathing is really important for getting good rhythm. You should fill your lungs with air before setting up to the ball, but make sure you breathe out before you hit, because relaxed muscles work much more effectively than tense ones. You will get more speed this way and the ball will go further. Never hold your breath.

Remember, swinging slower gives you more time to get your body and arms in harmony, generating more power.

The turn up to the top of the swing should be gradual and smooth – like winding up a coil – before increasing the power through the downswing.

Feel the resistance on the inside of your right leg and foot.

Don't hit at the ball, but accelerate through impact. Feel as though you are sweeping it off the tee.

Hover the clubhead to encourage a good clean takeaway. This should stop a jerky action.

→ Paul Casey
Six keys to solid contact

Pick your equipment

Technology has never been more important than it is now. Don't be frightened by it. If you want to be the best you've got to use it to your benefit. And you've got to have a driver in your hands which gives you confidence. Everyone is looking at their launch angles, spin rates and clubhead speeds. Make sure your equipment complements your game rather than the reverse.

When I play in the States, for instance, my driver has 9.5-degrees' loft, because I need the height and the carry. However, when I go over to Europe, where you are playing on courses with more of a linksy feel to them, then I switch down to a driver that is just 8.5 degrees to ensure that I get a bit more run on the ball.

Back to basics

1 Check your grip, set-up, ball position, alignment and posture, as many amateurs get these all wrong. The ball should ideally be positioned just opposite the inside of your left heel. This will help you engage in an upward sweeping action through impact, giving a good launch angle.

Hover

2 Hover the clubhead just above the ground at address. This will help ease tension in your hands and arms, and lead to a smooth rather than a twitchy takeaway.

High tees

3 You should tee the ball up high, so at least half the ball is above the clubface. This will enable you to sweep the ball away and not chop down on it.

Don't try and shape the driver. Just trust your swing technique and hit it. The driver is there for one reason – to launch the ball miles. If I don't want to do that I won't use it.

Driving

↑ ↑ ↑

Right-knee pivot

4 This is my only swing thought. I use my right knee as a fulcrum to turn around, and then I can fire off it. The right knee is the pivot around which the swing turns.

Focus on the strike

5 Concentrate on hitting the middle of the clubface. Under pressure, down the stretch, this is what I think about. Playing the final hole at The Belfry recently, I was concentrating on hitting the face. That fairway is large but I wasn't thinking about drawing the ball round the bunker. I knew if I hit the face and struck it well, it was safe.

Launch it

6 Don't try and shape your driver, just trust your technique and hit it. The driver is a launch club and is designed to hit the ball a long way – obvious, but worth repeating. When I've got my driver in hand, I pick a spot and launch it. If I want to work the ball, I'll use another club. The driver is there for one reason – to launch it miles. If I don't want that, I won't use it.

Posture and ball position correct

Hands and arms start to cock the club

Increase the torque factor as you turn the shoulders

Boom! Hit the ball flush

unwind to a full finish

and hold

Drill

Because I load up my right side so much, if I don't get back on my left side I'm in big trouble. So, one of the things I do with my coach Peter Kostis is to tee the ball down really really low. In order to hit this, there's just no way you can hang back on your right side.

Niclas Fasth
Get behind the ball

The key phrase with driving is get behind the ball. To help promote that in your set-up, move the ball forward in your stance, opposite the left heel. Everybody knows this. Then tee it up high. Everyone knows this, too. But people forget! In the swing make sure you stay behind the ball. Obviously your weight will shift on to your left foot in the downswing, but the head and upper body stay behind the ball. That enables you to hit it on the upswing. So it starts high, hopefully with not too much spin, and carries a long way.

 Get your head and upper body behind the ball at address.

2 Keep it that way in your back-swing …

Action point

You don't need to force the driver – make a smooth swing, catch it solid, and start it high. That promotes a long hit. The harder you try to hit it, the more backspin you put on it; so you hit it shorter!

Driving

↑ ↑ ↑

3 ... and then all the way into your downswing, until impact.

Learn the turn and easy release

The most important move in golf made simple

I often get asked how Tour pros hit the ball so far off the tee. It varies from player to player, but the fundamentals apply to everyone. The most important aspect of generating power is creating resistance in the backswing and you do this by getting a powerful shoulder turn. The greater width you can achieve in your swing, the more potential distance you can obtain.

Turn

Extend the arms to create width in your swing. Rotate the shoulders through 90 degrees so that your left shoulder is directly under your chin at the top of the backswing.

Weight

Transfer the weight from the left to the right side. Feel the resistance on the inside of the left knee as you turn away.

Takeaway

Slow and smooth. Keep the club tracking on the inside.

Flex

The right knee and angle of bend from the hip should be maintained throughout the swing. Don't straighten the right knee or try to 'stand up'.

Driving

↑ ↑ ↑

The easy release

Another drill to generate distance is the release of the hands. I use the split hands drill to help accentuate the feeling of releasing the club. You don't hit balls like this, it's simply to help get a feeling of allowing the right arm and hand to roll over through the hitting area. This movement creates a right to left shape on the ball that will add yards.

Separate the two hands so that the right hand is about a hand's width apart from the left on the shaft.

Feel like your right hand overtakes the left on the way down. The hands should roll over through impact.

Make a shorter backswing. Feel that the club is tracking on the inside on the backswing and downswing.

Padraig Harrington

Swing as far as your body lets you

Think short

There's a certain point in everyone's swing when their body is tight and they're ready to hit. If you extend past this, you lose all the elasticity in the muscles and ironically the extra swing causes a loss of power. If you stretch anything in your right side in your backswing then you are losing power.

Wrist-break

All you should be thinking about on your backswing is making sure the club breaks underneath your left thumb, which encourages the correct swing plane.

Turn, but don't sway

Everything in my left side turns: that's my left foot, knee, hip, torso, arm and hand. Many amateurs try to stand still.

Ball position

With big-headed woods and high tees, play the ball at least off your left toe to catch it on the upswing. The shot will go high, with minimal spin, and give you extra power in your drives.

Driving

↑ ↑ ↑

Finish balanced

You go to any golf club, and I guarantee you that more than two in every three-ball will lose their balance after hitting the ball. They'll take two or three steps after hitting their shot, or fall over backwards; so their weight isn't travelling through the ball at impact.

Solid platform

I keep my left foot planted on the ground because it gives me a solid platform.

Rotate the left arm

I like to rotate my left arm through impact, by holding the left wrist firm and rotating the right arm over the left.

Driving

↑ ↑ ↑

➔ Ian Woosnam
Swing at 85 per cent for more distance

As several players have already noted, striving for all-out power can be counterproductive when it comes to driving. It not only magnifies the effects of any defects in the swing, however slight these might be but can also actually reduce distance through mistiming the ball. Far better, sometimes, to hit within yourself, say at 85 per cent, and focus more on aspects of technique, such as a full shoulder turn, good tempo, smooth weight transfer and a balanced follow-through. The swing of Ian Woosnam illustrates all of these perfectly.

One of the requirements of a powerful strike is to maintain your height from start to finish, even if you have the diminutive stature of Woosie. This is best achieved by holding your chin off the chest at address and keeping it off until after impact.

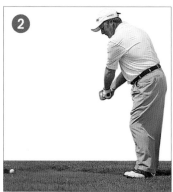

A useful thought to promote the necessary wide swing arc for distance is to start the clubhead back low and slow. It also helps to promote good tempo. Try to think that you're swinging at about 85 per cent.

A powerful and full backswing is determined by how far the body turns, rather than by how far the clubhead travels, and is achieved when the left shoulder points at the ball and the back faces the target.

Power in the downswing comes through uncoiling the left side, which pulls the club down to create leverage. This movement also clears the left side so there's plenty of room for the clubhead to travel on towards the target.

Instead of sliding your weight to the left side, which normally creates a push shot to the right, it's best to feel that you're turning your left side out of the way at the same time as you're transferring your weight to the front foot.

The proof of a powerful and balanced action can be found at the very end of the swing. A perfectly balanced follow-through sees the stomach facing the target and the weight on the outside of the left heel.

→ Pierre Fulke

Shorten your swing

A lot of people think that the longer your backswing, the further you hit the ball. But that's not usually the case. This is a common pitfall for many club golfers, especially when it comes to power clubs such as the driver. Often, the longer your swing gets, the less efficient it becomes. This was a problem I had in my own swing. I used to make a fairly poor shoulder turn, but I'd try to compensate for that by making a longer arm swing. Rather than helping me generate power, it cost me distance and accuracy.

So one of the things my coach Stefan Johansson and I have worked on in recent years is increasing my shoulder turn, while at the same time decreasing the length of my arm swing. The two keys – arm swing and body turn – work in harmony. As a result the club swings more on line through the hitting area, which helps eliminate bad shots and keeps the ball in play more of the time.

If you've got a driver in your hands and distance on your mind, resist the temptation to make a longer swing. Instead make the biggest shoulder turn you can, with the appropriate arm swing. Providing you complete a full wrist-hinge, you can generate all the power you need.

Get your arm swing and body turn working in harmony and the club will swing more on line through the hitting area.

A more controlled swing will help you retain balance – so important when trying to hit the ball further.

Make subtle changes to your swing and you'll start hitting straighter, more solid shots.

Driving

↑ ↑ ↑

→ Laura Davies
Pick a line for your drive

I never pick a point the same distance I'm trying to hit the ball. Instead, I always pick a point in the distance, and usually two points to aim between – like two trees a fairway distance apart. Then I focus on them… and probably go and block it into the bunker anyway!

⊕ **Greg Norman**
Glide the club away

The most important move when it comes to long driving is the takeaway, and when I'm all set for a big drive I try to 'glide' the club back from the ball for as long as possible. 'Low and slow' are the two key words.

A smooth and slow takeaway – gliding the club away from the ball – will help you to create width in the backswing.

Your head will move slightly in the backswing but at all times keep your focus on the ball.

A wide and stable stance is crucial when trying to create power in the swing.

Driving

↑ ↑ ↑

Corey Pavin

Shape your driver for extra distance

There are several different methods taught to draw the ball, but I find that the easiest way to get a right-to-left movement is to change my alignment at set-up. You can try this at the practice ground by placing a club on the ground aiming right of the target. Then turn the clubhead of your driver in so that it points at your target and grip the club. It should look shut at set-up. Now simply swing along the path of the iron on the ground. The ball should start to the right of your target and then draw back in. It's as easy as that.

Aim
Aim your feet, knees, hips, shoulders and forearms slightly right of the target. The further right you aim, the more exaggerated the draw you will create.

Swing
Make your normal swing, making sure you follow the directional path of the iron you've set down as a guideline.

Club
Close the face of the driver slightly so that it is aiming square to the target.

➔ Paul Eales

Take extra loft

I'm amazed more amateurs don't play safe with an iron when there's out-of-bounds or trees down the right-hand side of a fairway, especially those who tend to slice or fade their driver. I know it's not the way you want to play the game, but if you're trying to put together a decent score in a competition it's the best way to avoid disaster.

So give this strategy a try next time you play these tough holes. Instead of taking your driver, reach for a 4-iron. Compared to the driver, the extra loft on the clubface of a 4-iron creates more backspin and less sidespin, which means the ball is inclined to swerve much less through the air, and you don't end up in trouble down the right. If you're not too hot on your long irons, a 7-wood is a useful alternative.

Stay focused to be safe
One other important point: make sure you stay focused. An easy mistake to make, and this goes for professionals and amateurs alike, is letting the brain go to sleep when you opt for a lay-up shot of any kind. And when that happens it's so easy to hit your so-called safe shot into trouble, which is really annoying! So give it your fullest attention. That way you're more likely to execute the shot exactly as you imagined it.

Driving

↑ ↑ ↑

Choose your target

Approach this shot as if you're hitting a tee shot on a par three. Visualize a green in the middle of the fairway and hit your shot at that specific target. Don't aim just anywhere, because that's where you might hit it – anywhere!

Avoid the trouble

Once you've focused on your target in the middle of the fairway you will block out the trouble on the right-hand side. All you need do now is make a smooth and confident swing.

Hit a solid iron shot

Don't be obsessed by distance. On all but the very longest holes you'll be able to hit the green in three solid shots. So that's almost going to guarantee you a five. Better still, there's virtually no danger of you lashing your tee shot into trouble and racking up a seven or an eight.

→ → → # Through the Green

OK, so you've driven the ball and hopefully made it at least some distance down the fairway. But what next? Let's assume for the moment that you've split the fairway and are ideally placed for your next shot – unlikely, I know, but it's nice to dream once in a while! You'd like nothing more, wouldn't you, than for that dream to continue with a sweetly struck shot finding its way to the heart of the green, but how confident do you feel as you reach into your bag for a club? Does the thought of a long iron send shudders down your spine? How well can you judge the distance a middle iron will go? Are you able to plan ahead, visualizing the path you want the ball to take, or will you simply hit and hope? Absorb the lessons in this chapter concerning club selection, technique, visualization and strategy, and playing from fairway to green need hold no fears.

You needn't be afraid of your 3-iron

I think a lot of amateurs are scared of using their long irons because they think they are more difficult to hit than short irons. This is not the case. You only need to make a few subtle changes to your set-up to strike a 2- or 3-iron as purely, cleanly and accurately as your wedge.

Posture
Bend forwards from the hips and flex the knees, adopting an athletic position.

Grip
Grip the club lightly as though you are holding something delicate in your hands.

Backswing
Make a full 90-degree shoulder turn and transfer your weight on to the inside of the right heel. At the top of your backswing the weight should be 80 per cent on your right side.

Hands
Hands should be just ahead of the ball to encourage a clean, powerful downward strike into the back of the ball.

Ball position
This should be slightly forward of centre, inside your left heel.

Stance
The longer the club, the wider your stance. For a long iron your feet should be roughly shoulder-width apart. Do not take an overly wide stance as this will restrict your ability to turn your shoulders and transfer the weight.

Through the Green

⬆ ⬆ ⬆

Quick check

Always check your divot pattern. This is a good indication of how well you are attacking the shot. I know when I am swinging the club well as I will make little or no divot with my long irons – short, shallow divots are ideal. This is because there is so little loft on the club that it simply clips the surface of the turf. If you have a good tempo and sweep the club through impact rather than trying to 'hit' at the ball this should happen naturally.

Common mistakes

1. One of the biggest mistakes amateurs make is not completing their swing. This is usually the direct result of decelerating into the ball, causing them to hit the ground first and the shot to be heavy.

2. Swinging too hard or fast with an overswing (too long a backswing) will cause troubles. Keep the swing short and firm and your head steady.

Impact

Don't try and 'hit' the ball. The proper rotation of the body through the ball will ensure you get a good clean strike at impact.

Follow-through

To ensure that you get into a good follow-through position make sure you complete your shoulder turn, transfer your weight on to the left side and finish in a balanced pose.

A secure set-up for iron play

Getting your hands in a good position at set-up is fundamental
to ensuring a good shot. It's easy to practise in front of a mirror
so there are no excuses for adopting a poor position that could
lead to faults. Just follow these simple pointers.

Your grip should feel like
an extension of the arm.
You could hold a ruler
up against the line and
it would be straight.

Through the Green

↑ ↑ ↑ ↑

What not to do
The biggest mistake amateurs make is setting up with their hands behind the ball with a weak grip. This can lead to inconsistent strikes.

Before you grip the club, make sure you push your hands a couple of inches ahead of the ball. This will encourage a descending strike into the turf.

Don't scoop at the ball, bending the wrists – the natural loft on the club will get the ball airborne.

→ Vijay Singh
Make a smooth transition

One of the best tips I ever heard was to try to start your downswing at the same speed as you started your backswing. This helps you make a smooth start down, which encourages all the moving parts of your swing to work together. If you rush that first move down, you lose synchronization and with that your chances of hitting a solid shot are considerably reduced.

The transition from backswing to downswing is one of the most important moves you will make. So don't rush it.

Too many amateur golfers lunge at the ball. Just let it get in the way of a smooth swing.

↑
↑
↑

Bernhard Langer

Picture the shot before you play it

After making a practice swing, I walk behind the ball and visualize as vividly as I can the flight of the ball. I often then pick an intermediate target a few feet in front of the ball to help me with my alignment.

1 Stand behind the ball.

2 Size up where you need to hit it to avoid hazards etc. and be in optimum position for the next shot.

3 Visualize the flight of the ball in your mind's eye.

4 Choose a target close to the ball to aid alignment.

5 Play the shot.

Mid-irons

Mid-irons are probably the easiest clubs to hit, with the most margin for error. A logical way to look at the technique is to think of the shot as being right in the middle of the wedge and driver, with the ball in the centre of the stance.

1 Chin up – always a good start.

2 Hands directly under shoulders is a useful check-point.

3 Spine should feel relatively straight, to avoid hunching.

Through the Green

↑
↑
↑

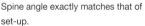

4 Spine angle exactly matches that of set-up.

5 Acceleration through impact should feel smooth, not forced.

6 Always set out to finish in balance; it promotes good rhythm.

➔ Vijay Singh
Picture my rhythm

When I was an amateur I modelled my swing on Tom Weiskopf. After that, I copied anyone who I thought was doing something well. I've read a lot of instruction books since then and picked out things I considered relevant to my game. It can help.

For instance, if you feel your swing is too quick, or you're in a pressure situation when you want to avoid that happening, then it may well help if you picture my golf swing. I'm sure you've seen me hit plenty of shots on TV and I like to think it's one of the smoothest swings in the game. Having this kind of image in your mind can promote a smooth rhythm in your own swing. And since most bad shots hit under pressure are a result of swinging too quickly, it's well worth giving it a try.

If you're under pressure, think of my swing to keep your rhythm smooth. Just make sure you commit yourself to accelerating the club through the ball.

As a general rule, if you can't hold your finish you are swinging too quickly.

Nick Dougherty
Sharpen your focus

Golfers generally pick a target that is too big. They will probably aim at the green, rather than picking an exact point on the green to aim at. The sharper your focus is, the better results you will get.

On this hole, all the trouble is on the front left of the green. So I would advise players to aim at a point on the centre-right side of the green. Also, remember to allow a little bit extra for the wind. Here the flag is blowing to the left so the wind is off the right and I would aim a bit further right to allow for the carry in the air.

Draw an imaginary line from the target along the ground to the ball.

Hold your club up and point it at the target like a gun.

Set up to the ball and aim the club at the imaginary line. Focus on that point – not the pin.

➔ **Padraig Harrington**

Grip down on approach shots

It's very rare that you need to hit a shot full out from 130 to 150 yards – yet that's a common mistake among amateurs. Most club golfers would do much better by easing off now and again, and the way to do that is to grip the club down the shaft a little.

This makes it a lot easier to hit a nice, controlled shot, especially in the wind, as it takes spin off the ball and moves it through the breeze rather than ballooning upwards or deviating left or right.

When I go down the shaft I feel it's a mental key to tell me I've got plenty of club in my hands, and to focus on making a smooth, rhythmical swing. It tends to take five yards off my normal shot, and the ball doesn't bite as much on the green, but overall I feel I can control the distance better.

Grip down the shaft for greater control.

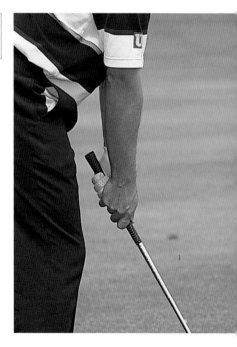

⬆ ⬆ ⬆

Focus on making a nice, smooth and rhythmical swing.

Swing within yourself on approach shots

Just as swinging within yourself leads to greater accuracy off the tee, so the same principle can help you hit more greens in regulation. A comfortable pace of swing has its roots in knowing how far you hit each iron, because mentally that knowledge removes the temptation to thrash at the ball. You have a yardage, you simply pick the right club. You don't have to work to an exact distance but you should be able to calculate a yardage for each club give or take 10 per cent. And if we're talking about hitting greens, that's good enough. These yardages are easy to work out. All you need is a bag of balls and a bit of spare time.

At 6ft 1in Justin Rose makes a good job of adopting a comfortable address position. Note his spine angle – bent forward just enough to allow the hands and arms to hang down freely and with some clearance from his body.

A good, no-nonsense takeaway. Justin makes it look so easy – the hands and arms swing the club back, as the shoulders and torso begin to turn. Notice the clubface position, with the toe pointing at the sky – that's perfectly neutral.

A good takeaway makes it much easier to swing to the top and get there in good shape, and this proves it. From halfway into his backswing all Justin needs to do is keep turning his shoulders and make sure his arm swing stays in tune.

↑ ↑ ↑

To hit more greens, you can't rush the move from backswing to down-swing. Justin makes a very smooth transition and that's the big differ-ence from the majority of club golfers, who often rush this crucial phase of the swing. Start down at the same speed you took the club back – that will do the trick.

The clubhead is travelling so fast that the image you see of Justin at impact is best described as a position within motion – in many ways a product of what happened earlier in the swing. Notice how Justin's spine angle is the same as at address – this is a sure sign of an efficient rotary body action.

Note how the right arm at this stage of the follow-through is at the same angle as the left arm at the top of the backswing. That's the sign of a balanced, on-plane swing whereby the hands and arms work in synch with the body motion. It's the recipe for a succession of solidly struck, straight iron shots.

Know your distance and don't force it

One of the things I think the dual-image below reveals about my swing is how totally under control it is. And therein lies one of the keys to being a better pitcher of the ball – that all-important word, control.

Firstly, it's important you establish how far you hit each of your pitching clubs – and I'm talking comfortable swings here, not flat-out thrashes. Just a dozen or so shots at the range with each club will give you a good idea of distances. Then you need to swing within those limits on the golf course. Never force a pitch shot. Know your range and stick to it – that's what I do. For me the perfect distance for

a pitch shot with my 56-degree wedge is 95 yards. If it's much more than that to the flag, or if there's a stiff breeze in my face, I take more club. It's as simple as that. This is the sort of approach you need to take. Make a comfortable swing every time and let the loft on the club do the talking.

How to hit greens with your mind

A great way to hit more greens requires a simple shift in strategy; just aim at the centre of the green on every hole you play. Resist the temptation to attack pins, except with the pitching clubs. Tour pros adopt this strategy a lot more than most casual viewers realize and the club golfer would do well to copy them. It's a smart option that can only benefit your scoring potential. Not only do your good shots still find the green, so too do your slightly wayward shots. And that in itself makes a huge difference.

Spot the tension – you can't! There's a wonderful sense of free-flowing movement about this image. It's definitely a swing, not a hit, and heading for the middle of the green.

→ → → Bunker Play

If there's one hazard on the golf course that sends most amateurs into paroxysms of fear it's a bunker or sand trap. And it's not just the cavernous pot bunkers of St Andrews, Troon or Carnoustie that create such fear – a seemingly innocuous patch of sand down your local municipal can have an equally dramatic effect. Most players think they know what to do yet are unable to do it, and therein lies the problem, for when you've tried umpteen times to thrash your way out of a trap, each time to be met with failure, a mystique inevitably develops about the shot. Yet, like all aspects of the game, success is simply down to correct technique. Look after the basics and the rest will take care of itself. The tips in this chapter will enable you, next time you find the sand – whether it be on the fairway or around the green – to find your way out with confidence and at least limit the damage, if not eliminate it altogether.

The controlled splash shot

I've played golf with many amateurs and bunker play is usually the weakest part of their game. Rather than looking to get up-and-down from the sand, most players will accept any shot that gets them out of the bunker, without even thinking about playing for position. But with a bit of practice the controlled splash shot can be played to any point on the green, allowing you to position the ball. Just look at the distance to the point where you want to land the ball – this will determine how much loft you give the clubface.

Bunker Play

↑ ↑ ↑

Open clubface
For a short shot like this, I will open up the clubface a lot and lay it almost flat.

Aim left

My body is aiming left (open) and I have good balance, with a little more weight on my left foot – this helps take the club down into the sand.

Less sand or more

The amount of sand I take depends on the distance. On longer shots, the clubface and body will be squarer and I will take less sand. For shorter shots, I will open the face and body, and take more sand.

→ Tiger Woods
Classic bunker technique

Bunker play used to be Tiger's biggest weakness, but that didn't last long. His technique is now classic, his execution of sand shots pretty much flawless. At the heart of Tiger's recovery play from sand is visualization. Like all good bunker players, he has in his mind a very precise picture of the intended trajectory, landing area, and roll of the ball. When he gets into the sand, fulfilling those criteria is all he's focused on. It's something that a lot of amateurs would do well to copy. It helps focus the mind on a positive outcome, and therefore stops you thinking negatively.

Follow through
Gary Player, the greatest sand player of them all, says 'always follow through in bunkers'. Tiger does. So should you.

Bunker Play

↑ ↑ ↑

(Above, left) You have to hinge your wrists in the backswing to promote the ideal descending attack in the downswing.

(Above, right) No rocket science here. Tiger opens his stance and the clubface at address and then swings the club down and through along his aim line.

(Right) Tiger controls distance through the speed of his swing and, as a direct result of that, the length of his follow-through.

Power through sand

The most common cause of the fluffed bunker shot is a deceleration into the sand. This causes the club to lose power, too much sand is taken and the shot is fluffed. The best bunker players in the world are always the most positive ones. I like to think of the analogy of driving through the sand. This is particularly relevant for the longer bunker shot. To get a little extra distance just make a less steep backswing and drive your hands and arms forwards, allowing the club to sweep on a shallow path through the sand. The ball should come out a little lower, carry further, and run out and up to the hole.

Body position
At address my knees point forwards, which puts my weight on the left foot, while keeping my head above the ball. During the back-swing I leave my legs in the same position they were at address.

Impact
Feel like you are driving through the sand, accelerating hard.

Follow-through
Aim for a three-quarter length follow-through for added control.

Joakim Haeggman
The plugged lie

There are two ways of tackling the problem of a buried ball. For both, place your weight towards the left foot. This weight shift gives you a steeper swing plane, which allows you to get through the sand better. Professionals tend to use an open blade, which results in a higher flight and a softer landing. If you are a club player you don't have the clubhead speed to use this method. As the club hits the sand it opens so you should shut down the loft a little to make sure it doesn't open too much. This gives you enough dig to get through the sand.

Pick the club up steeply

Quick tip
The sand wedge is made so that it bounces, so for a plugged lie it is actually better for a lot of amateurs to take a pitching wedge.

Better players should open the face wide. Average players will benefit from a closed clubface.

Hover the club a couple of inches behind the ball and aim to hit into the sand at this point. Your weight should favour the left side at address.

The doughnut

The most common mistake I see people making is trying to scoop the ball out of the bunker. This causes them to get too wristy and hit the sand either too early, causing a fat and leaving the ball in, or too late, causing a thin and sending the ball over the back of the green. Drawing a ring around the ball when you practise takes your attention away from hitting the golf ball to hitting through the sand.

Draw a ring a few inches wide around your golf ball. Aim to hit into the sand at this point.

Open the clubface so that it aims at the target and hover the club over the back line of the doughnut ring.

Remember
Always be aggressive with this shot. The sensation should be that you are hitting the ball at the top of the flagstick, not short of it. Don't forget the bunker is a hazard. Don't get too cheeky with the shot. Just take your medicine and make sure you get out.

Bunker Play

↑ ↑ ↑ ↑

84

You should be trying to hit the whole of the doughnut – and everything within it – out on to the green.

Shuffle your feet into the sand and aim left of the target.

Pick the club up steeply on the back-swing.

What not to do
Don't stand square to the ball. Stand open and open the clubface. This allows you to swing across the ball, giving an aggressive angle of attack into the sand.

Accelerate through the sand.

→ Ernie Els

Be more aggressive on an upslope in the sand

Every picture tells its own story and this one of me at the US Open is no exception. To me, the message that really comes out is that you have to be so much more aggressive when you're on an upslope in a bunker. I mean, just look how much sand is coming out with the ball. That itself tells you the amount of speed the clubhead is carrying into the sand.

Whenever you're on an upslope, settle the majority of your weight on the lower leg and keep it there during the swing. Also make sure the clubface is square rather than open. Now make a longer swing than you would from a flat lie and, as I say, be much more aggressive in the downswing. You almost want to feel that you're hitting the shot twice as hard from an upslope as you would from a decent lie on the flat. One thing's for sure: you can fly the ball right up to the hole knowing for certain that it will stick in the green like a dart in a board.

→ **Davis Love III**
Hit high and short from sand

This is a tough sand shot, but with a little know-how and some well-thought-out practice, it's one that you'll find as enjoyable as it is useful. For your first clue as to how to play it, focus on the position of Davis Love's hands in the picture below as he manufactures this shot at the 1997 US Open. The right hand works under, cupping the left wrist as he literally slides the clubhead through the sand under the ball. Also note how the arms have barely swung through, but the club has travelled a long way. It's this steep, wristy action that delivers lots of loft at impact.

Before you even start your swing, though, hold your hands lower at address. This encourages a slightly steeper swing plane, which is ideal for this shot. Also open the clubface and your stance a little more than you would normally.

⊜ **Lee Westwood**

Blitz the fairway bunker

The important thing with a fairway bunker shot is to hit the ball cleanly, without hitting the sand first – that way you'll be able to reach the green or at least move the ball a good distance down the fairway.

I always tend to take one club more than I would otherwise need because I'm going to grip down the shaft a bit and that reduces distance. So if it's a 7-iron, take a 6-iron instead.

1 Work your feet into the sand to give yourself a firm base and move the ball back towards the centre of your stance. This will help you hit the ball cleanly rather than the club going into the sand.

2 Because your feet are sat down in the sand, you will need to grip down the shaft. This will also give you more control over the shot.

3 I tend to put a little more weight on my left foot and try not to shift my weight back to the right foot during the backswing. Again, this will help you make a clean contact with the ball. Sometimes I will make a slightly shorter swing to ensure a good strike, but essentially you should make your normal swing. If you do all that, you should hit the ball out nice and cleanly.

→ **Ian Garbutt**

The 60–80-yard bunker shot

Lots of par-fives have bunkers positioned close to where your second shot will land. That's no coincidence – they're there to catch you out. You're going to hit the sand from time to time, which means facing one of those tough 60–80-yard bunker shots. Follow these simple rules of engagement and you'll make a decent fist of it every time.

Bunker Play ↑ ↑ ↑ ↑

1 First, don't automatically reach for your sand wedge. That's a common error with the mid-range bunker shot. Instead, take your pitching wedge. A little less loft will help you get the ball up around the green.

2 Next, place the ball in the centre of your stance and nudge your hands ahead of the clubhead.

3 Keep your rhythm and accelerate smoothly into your downswing so you don't lose your footing. You'll take some sand at impact, but the crucial thing is that it happens after you strike the ball. Concentrate on 'ball-then-sand' contact.

4 Granted this is more unforgiving than a shot from the fairway, because if you catch it even slightly heavy you'll come up well short. But that's no reason to panic. Just focus on the points I've demonstrated and you'll be impressed with the results.

→ Joakim Haeggman
Ball above your feet

The key to this shot is getting into the slope. If the ball is above me I tend to move backwards (away from the ball) a little so I can cope with the slope. On this sort of shot it is important not to change your body angles; if you do, you rise up too much. You want to hit *with* the slope rather than trying to fight it. Playing off a slope in a bunker is very similar to playing a ball above your feet in that you need to adjust where you aim. Point your clubface and body a little bit right and the drag will take the ball towards the target.

Aim right of the target as the drag of the slope will take the ball to the left.

Set yourself up slightly further away from the ball to give yourself room to swing around the slope.

Keep your weight down through impact.

Golf Tips from the Pros 91

➜ ➜ ➜ The Short Game

According to the professionals, if there's one aspect of the game that lets down most amateurs it's the short game. Never mind crashing the ball off the tee or sending a long iron soaring down the fairway – what counts most in terms of securing a good score is those little shots around the green. Across the years it's been that special ability to get the ball close that has separated the greats from the also-rans, tournaments being won or lost on the strength of one chip. Your ambitions may be more modest, but getting the short game right can mean the difference between being a hacker and scratch golfer. Learn in this chapter from some of the finest exponents of the art of chipping, and see your handicap swiftly tumble.

⊖ Scott Drummond

Perfect pitching

Keeping your technique simple is the key to short game consistency. My shots from 40 yards used to be the inconsistent area of my game. When I've played well it's because I've hit a lot of greens in regulation and not had to make up and down to save par. When I have played poorly it's because my short game has let me down. So along with my long-term coach Keith Williams I decided that to take my game to the next level required a complete overhaul of my greenside technique. My short game has always been based on feel rather than sound technique. I've played with a very wristy action and when I'm on song this is very effective, but when the timing is out it's unreliable. I've altered the technique to limit my hand and wrist action and developed one simple method that can be applied to all shots around the green. It's easy to learn; here's how it works.

Remember
Even on a bad day the best players in the world have a short game that will save them shots. To be this good you need a reliable, consistent technique, and my method of pitching ensures control.

Shoulder turn
From the solid central chest position it is easy to turn just the shoulders through the shot.

Chest
The centre of the chest is over the ball.

Bounce
Allow the natural loft and bounce of your wedge to do the work for you. Don't let the hands manipulate it.

Sound set-up

1 To hit a lower shot simply bring the ball back slightly, and for a higher trajectory push it forward. My aim is to get the chest over the ball at address, the left shoulder sitting just below the chin. This helps me to turn the shoulders, preventing the arms getting trapped close to the body in the downswing.

Use the bounce

2 As a wristy player my tendency was to lead with the arms into the shot. This would cause the leading edge of the club to cut down steeply into the ground. Now I am trying to let the wedge do the work for me, by allowing the bounce on the sole of the club to come more effectively into my pitch shots. You can only do this from a shallower swing plane.

Backswing

3 My arm swing feels slightly longer in the backswing than it was before because my body is turning more. There is less independent wrist action. My key swing thought is to turn my chest over the ball as I take the club back. Rather than pick the club up steeply I take it away wide and on a shallower plane.

Length and pace

4 It is important to get consistent swing length and pace for these control shots. I work my arms and body together, turning with my shoulders so that I create a wider, shallower swing action, which gives a crisper strike.

Angle of attack

5 Rather than swinging down steeply into the shot I have shallowed my angle of attack into the ball. My right shoulder stays higher, giving more room for the arms and upper body to work in harmony.

Constant loft

6 To play this shot effectively keep the loft of your wedge constant through impact. Don't allow your hands to manipulate the club open or shut. Play the shot with your upper body; the arms and shoulders lead.

The half wedge

In terms of mechanics, this shot is the complete opposite of the driver. With the wedge you need to be ahead of the ball so you can hit down on it. You have to generate a steeper angle of approach to become a good wedge player. Be aware of how you stand to the ball. That's where a lot of amateurs go wrong. They set up in a way that feels comfortable, but if you want to be ahead of the ball at impact, it makes sense to pre-set that into your address. That's why you should move the ball back and the weight a little bit to the left.

The Short Game

⬆ ⬆ ⬆ ⬆

1 Feel like you're in front of the ball at address.

2 Then maintain that same feeling in the backswing.

3 This allows you to strike down into the ball.

4 And that's the way you generate the correct flight and spin.

5 Note how the head stays over the point of impact throughout.

Action point

These are difficult shots, but with practice, you can improve. If you can discipline yourself to ignore the driver when you go to the range, and instead spend the time hitting different length wedge shots, you'll be amazed at the transformation which filters into your game.

The short pitch

Most amateurs get into a complete mess, technique-wise, when they're faced with a shot that is neither a chip nor a full pitch. It's somewhere in between the two, and frankly, that's pretty hard to deal with for a lot of golfers. The secret lies not in any complicated, fancy swing theories, but in simple no-nonsense fundamentals applied with authority, as illustrated by Woods. With a bit of practice, anyone can do that.

1 Such good posture. But look also at the slightly open stance and open clubface. They're just as important for this kind of shot.

The Short Game

↑ ↑ ↑ ↑

98

2 One sentence sums this up. Turn your body as you swing your hands and arms back. Oh, and add a little wrist-hinge for good measure.

3 The left arm leads the club into the hitting area, and the angles established in the wrists are maintained to ensure a crisp downward blow.

4 Keep your nerve, and your rhythm. Accelerate the clubhead smoothly down and through impact. Let the club create loft and don't flick at the ball.

5 As in the backswing, the follow-through reflects the importance of turning the body as you swing the hands and arms through.

Make your ball dance

People think that generating backspin on the ball is a mystical, magical thing that only Tour pros can do. The truth is everyone can put spin on the ball. It's all about getting a good strike. Here are a few tips to help you get the ball to stop on the greens.

Come clean: Make sure the grooves of your club are clean from soil and grass. With dirt in the grooves of your club there is resistance between the ball and the club so there will be less interaction to help generate the spin.

Hit it hard: Commit to the shot. A positive blow into the back of the ball is much more likely to impart spin than a gentle hit.

Golf ball: Don't forget it's not all about the way you swing. Using a high-spin ball will help get the control you're looking for.

Remember: It's much easier to get your wedges and short irons to spin than your long irons. This is because you are making a steeper swing with the short irons, they have more loft and the club is coming in on a steeper angle of attack down into the back of the ball.

Hands ahead

A slightly forward hand position, encouraged by moving the ball back in your stance, will help generate that descending blow into the back of the ball.

Ball position

Place the ball a tad further back in your stance than normal for this type of shot. It helps you hit down into the back of the ball, encouraging extra backspin.

The Short Game

↑ ↑ ↑ ↑

Phillip Price
Swivel your eyes; don't lift your head

One of the main reasons some amateurs chip poorly is that they alter the angles in their posture during the swing. This makes it virtually impossible to produce a consistent strike. Often it's because they lift their head a little too soon or stand up through impact. Either way, lots of mishits are the result. To avoid lifting the head and body I swivel my eyes without moving my head as I swing through, just like I do for a putt. This helps me to maintain my original head height and spine angle, which gives me more consistency on my ball strike.

(Right) Correct: the eyes swivel to follow the ball flight.

(Below) Incorrect: the head has lifted up.

Get set to chip

If you get your set-up wrong, you've had it, so here are a few things to keep in mind. Put your hands forward, so the shaft of the club and your left arm are pretty much in a straight line. Settle your weight on the left foot, and put the ball back in the stance a little. Your arms and shoulders should form a triangle and in doing that you've basically pre-set your impact, which means you don't have to do anything fancy in your swing.

If you set up poorly, though, you have to make compensations in your swing to get into a good position at impact. That usually involves a lot of hand and wrist action, possibly body movement too. It makes the shot harder to execute properly. So pay attention to those seemingly boring set-up details. They count more than you think.

1 Arms and shoulders form a triangle.

2 Hand position: ahead of the ball.

3 Ball position: just back of the centre of the stance.

If you set up poorly, you have to make compensations in your swing to get into a good position at impact.

The Short Game

→ Bernhard Langer
One shot for every chip

Most pros at the top of the game keep the technique for chipping essentially the same for every shot, altering the club in order to give themselves the appropriate loft to suit each situation – maximum loft when there's very little green to work with; less loft when there's more room to run the ball along the ground. Bernhard Langer is one of the world's finest exponents of this art and is a far better chipper than he is given credit for. Bernhard's choice of chipping clubs will tend to revolve primarily around the 9-iron, pitching wedge and lob wedge. The reason only the most lofted clubs get a look-in is simply down to practicality. On Tour the greens are very fast (usually around 10.5 to 11 on the stimpmeter). Also the pins tend to be cut in tight positions, so combine those two factors and there's usually a far greater need for height and spin than there is for roll. Mind you, whenever a long chip and run is required you'll see players like Langer switch to something like a 7-iron in order to get the ball running up the green. It's the smart option.

Put most of your weight on the front foot, position the ball back in your stance, and have your hands forward.

Choose a club to suit the situation – maximum loft when there's little green to work with; less loft when you want the ball to roll.

Focus on the spot where you want the ball to land.

The low pitch and run

In general if the green is fairly flat then the safest shot to play is the running shot. Select a club with less loft, such as a 7- or 8-iron, and play the ball a little further back in your stance. I always use a pretty narrow stance as it feels most comfortable. I push my hands a little bit ahead, but keep the clubhead square. I also grip a little bit further down for added control. I always aim to pitch the ball the same distance. To hit the ball further I simply take a less lofted club.

The Short Game

↑ ↑ ↑ ↑

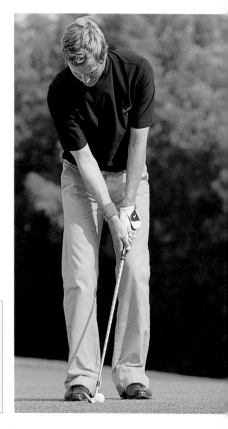

Set-up
Open the stance slightly. Grip down a little for control. Ball position is a little further back, towards your back foot.

Backswing

(Left) Swing slowly with less wrist-break, no further than waist high. The swing path should be wider and flatter than normal.

Follow through

(Below, left and right) Keep your left wrist firm through impact. The follow-through should mirror the backswing.

Expert chipping

One of the things I think is important about a short pitch or chip shot is to grip right down on the club (picture A). For one thing this increases your feel for the shot. More importantly, though, it effectively shortens your swing arc so you can be a little more positive and accelerate the clubhead through the ball without fear of over-shooting the target.

I find that the tendency for a lot of average players is to grip the club long (picture B), just as they would to hit a full shot. Then they make way too long a backswing and have to decelerate coming into the ball. That's risky. Sometimes you can catch it fat, other times you might skull it over the green. It's tough to get it right when your swing is so long for such a short shot.

Try playing it in the same way as demonstrated in the sequence of pictures (right).

The Short Game

↑ ↑ ↑

Grip down the club so that your right hand is virtually on the steel of the shaft.

Your normal grip should look something like this. Notice the difference.

(Above, left) By gripping down the club, you'll automatically have a shorter arc. Your swing will feel more compact and you'll get a more consistent strike.

(Above, right) You will also get more speed through the ball, which is what you want, even though it's a short shot.

(Left) Go out there and practise the shot. Trust me, it will save you a bunch of shots every round of golf you play.

Jim Furyk

Limit your backswing to strike delicate chips

This sort of short chip shot is often a big problem for amateurs. In my view it comes down to the fact that they take the club back too far in the backswing. That means they either decelerate in the downswing, hitting the ball fat or thin, or they go ahead and make solid contact, which means they knock it way past the pin. It leads to so many wasted shots.

From close range, think of the ideal chipping technique as pretty much like a putting stroke. You want the swing to be fairly short and compact, and you want it to have some rhythm. And importantly, you don't want to take the club back any further than you must; a foot or two is ample. Then you can accelerate through the ball and make solid contact without fear of overshooting the pin. When you're only trying to carry the ball five yards, it's so easy to take a long swing and then quit on it.

Finally, try to think of your follow-through being at least as long as your backswing, maybe even longer. That will help make doubly sure that you accelerate through the ball.

The Short Game

I want to carry the ball five yards only and let it run to my caddie. A sand wedge is the club.

The key to a clean strike, as I see it, is to make just a short, compact backswing.

This encourages good acceleration and solid contact. With practice it's really very simple to execute.

→ Vijay Singh
Chip dead every time

The mechanics of this shot are really simple. Just keep everything basic, don't do anything fancy. I start by focusing on where I want the ball to land. Decide your club depending on how far you want the ball to run out. The shorter the shot the more lofted the club you'll need to use. Play the ball towards the middle of your stance, and keep the hands ahead. The key to playing this shot well is to get a good hands-and-arms swing. I just accelerate the clubhead through the ball, letting the loft of the club do all the work for me and then allowing the ball to run out towards the pin.

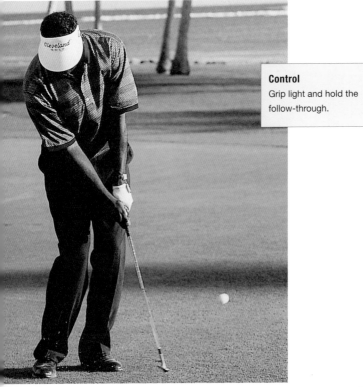

Control
Grip light and hold the
follow-through.

The soft-landing chip

Here's how to hit a delicate chip shot out of a bad lie, without falling into the trap of duffing it short of the flag.

There are times around the green, especially when you find yourself in an awkward lie, when a pitch and run shot or ordinary chip simply will not work. What's needed instead is a chip that rises quickly and comes down soft, with little if any roll. It's a delicate shot, but get it right and you will avoid the embarrassment of either shooting the ball well past the flag or of duffing it short. The required technique is perfectly illustrated by Tiger Woods, a master of the craft.

1 Early wrist-break in the takeaway is essential, as it sets the club on a slightly steeper arc.

2 Keep hands ahead of the ball to guarantee a downward strike as you accelerate into impact.

3 Hands still ahead of the clubhead. This keeps the face open and lofts the ball with more height than there is forward momentum.

Pick the right club

The most important thing when pitching is club selection. If you choose
the wrong club you reduce the chances of making a good shot. Your
selection will depend entirely on the situation. If it is downwind, you
should take a more lofted club, like a sand wedge. But if it is into the
wind, you can take a pitching wedge, or sometimes even a 9-iron.

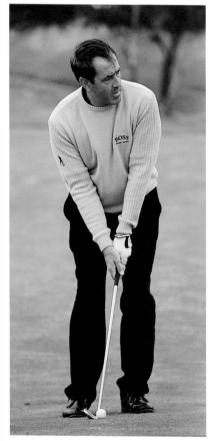

The Short Game

↑ ↑ ↑ ↑

Body position
Aim your body slightly
left of the target.

Ball position
For a short pitch shot,
keep the ball pretty
much in the centre of
your stance.

You should adopt the same set-up and use the same swing that you would for a full shot with that club. To regulate the length of the shot simply alter the length of your backswing and the speed of the club. The faster and longer you swing, the further the ball will go.

For longer pitches you may need to make your stance squarer and put less weight on the left side, but the swing is essentially the same. Keep the shot simple.

Clubface
Aim the club-face square to the target.

Weight
Keep the weight pre-dominantly on the left side – your front foot.

Eliminate the duff chip

Dunch, duff, heavy; it's all the same thing. The clubhead hits the ground before making contact with the ball. It can happen anywhere, but it's on chip shots that the shame is most acutely felt, because the ball barely makes it out of your shadow. As such, it's about as damaging to your ego as it is to your score. This bad shot comes about solely as a result of trying to help the ball into the air. All the signs are there at address – the weight leaning back and the hands behind the ball, which is too far forward in the stance.

Right

Make sure your hands are in front of the ball and that your weight slightly favours your left side. Your grip should be soft and your stance slightly 'open' – aiming a few feet left of the target to allow the club to swing more easily through impact on the correct path.

Wrong

Hands are behind the ball and the weight favours the right foot.

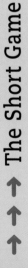

The Short Game

↑ ↑ ↑

Make sure your weight favours the front foot. Nudge your hands slightly ahead of the ball. Your stroke for short chips should be similar to a smooth and pendulum-like putting stroke.

Soft grip, weight forward and hands forward.

Chip with your centre of gravity over the ball

I play with amateurs every week in pro-ams, and usually two out of three of them struggle with their short games, and 99 per cent have the same fault. It's unbelievably simple to solve.

When amateurs are chipping, they come into the ball wanting to lift the ball into the air and their body is moving backwards as they are hitting the ball. This means they will always strike the ground before the ball.

Instead, try getting your centre of gravity (your sternum or breastbone) right over the ball, and you will find you suddenly start striking the ball sweetly. It doesn't then matter whether you break your wrists or not; this technique will work.

When you rock back, everything will break down.

Here my weight is right over the ball.

⊕ Seve Ballesteros
How to play the greenside chip

It's one of the most common short-game scenarios. Your approach has run off the side of a slightly elevated green, down a bank and into fringe grass. What's the best way of getting back on to the green and up beside the hole? Seve reveals all.

Club choice
The first thing to do is to think about which club to use. If you take an 8-iron the ball may take off low and hit the bank immediately in front of you. So make sure you choose a club with enough loft – I frequently use a pitching wedge.

It's important to try and visualize the shot – how the ball is going to come out of the lie and where you want to land it.

Take into consideration where the ball will break once it lands – just as you would with a putt. I look for a flat area and then concentrate on landing the ball on that spot.

The technique is the same with all my chip shots. I address the ball more or less in the middle of my stance, but my feet and body are aiming slightly left. The clubface, though, is square to where I want the ball to go.

Grip down the shaft a little and hold the club softly. Take the club back, then let the weight of the head do the work coming through, keeping the clubface square.

➡ Alastair Forsyth

Chip putt from the fringe

This shot virtually didn't exist 10 years ago. Now nearly all the pros are playing it. It's basically a putt-chip with a 5-wood or a rescue club, a seemingly odd combination that actually makes perfect sense when you get down to it. It's the ideal shot when you've got a fluffy lie just off the green with lots of green between your ball and the pin.

From here it would be easy to catch it a bit heavy with a conventional chip and leave the ball halfway. With a 5-wood the clubhead just glides through the grass around the ball. It's what you might call an anti-duff chip shot.

With a 5-wood the clubhead just glides through the grass around the ball. It's what you might call an anti-duff chip shot.

The Short Game

↑ ↑ ↑ ↑

Approach it like a putt

1 This shot is so easy to play – it's exactly like a putt. Choke down on the grip, so the fingers on your right hand are almost touching the shaft. This makes the shaft shorter and more manageable. Then adopt your regular putting stance and grip.

Keep the clubhead low

2 Swing the club back and through as if you were hitting a long putt. The clubhead stays pretty low to the ground throughout the stroke, collecting the ball on its way through the hitting area.

Carry the fringe

3 The 5-wood has just enough loft to carry the ball over the rough. Once it hits the ground it runs exactly like a putt because there's no spin on the ball.

Practise the shot

4 The thing to remember is that the ball comes off the face pretty 'hot' – the first few times you play it you'll probably over-shoot the target. With a few practice shots you'll get used to the pace of the ball – from then on it's easy to judge and impossible to duff!

Don't push your luck

This is a handy shot – one I've played many times in tournaments – but it soon becomes foolhardy if you take just a few steps further into the rough. Remember, there's very little loft on a 5-wood, so the ball will carry only a yard or two before it hits the ground. If the ball lands in rough, it gets snagged up and doesn't run. So if there's more than a yard of rough between you and the green, you're best off playing a conventional chip.

The grip

For this shot you should use your normal putting grip. Note that the hands are near the shaft of the club.

→ → → Trouble Spots

Sooner or later on the golf course you're going to find trouble. It's not so much a case of 'if' as 'when', and so often that proves to be all too early and often in a round. You've already seen in Chapter 4 how to deal with bunkers, but there are plenty more problems lying in wait to destroy a promising round. You can't do much if you land in water, of course, apart from take a drop and learn from your mistake, but what of the rough or trees, not to mention those awkward situations that can take you by surprise, just when you think you've played a good shot: finding yourself, perhaps in a divot, or up against the fringe, or with a nasty hanging lie? This chapter offers invaluable tips for dealing with such eventualities; tips that may just help you keep that promising round together.

Take your medicine

Scoring well isn't all about hitting fairways and greens. It is also about making the most of a bad situation. It might sound obvious, but the one thing you should do when you hit a bad shot into trouble is to make sure you take your medicine and get out. Unless you've been incredibly fortunate to find a good lie and have a clear route to the green it is simply not worth taking on a risky shot. It is much wiser to chip out sideways back on to the fairway and at least give yourself a chance of getting up and down to save par. Be sensible; don't be a hero unless you have no other choice.

Club selection
Check for overhanging branches or anything that may affect your swing. Then choose a club that is the most lofted for the situation, but that will ensure the ball avoids any trees on the way out.

The shot
Play out of trouble with a chip shot and keep it all nice and simple. Play to get back in position.

Trouble Spots

↑ ↑ ↑

→ Justin Rose
Playing from tight lies

A chip off a tight lie is not hard if you keep it simple. Put the ball back in your stance, opposite your right foot, and have your weight leaning forwards. That helps you hit down on the ball and get a nice, crisp strike.

I use my lob wedge. It has very little bounce on the sole of the club, which helps me strike the ball cleanly. If you use a club with a lot of bounce, like a regular sand wedge, there's a danger of the clubhead skipping into the middle of the ball and you 'knife' it like a bullet across the green!

One final point to remember, let the loft on the club do its job – don't try to help the ball into the air.

Coping with the rough

There are two categories of shot from the rough – distance shots where you're trying to advance the ball as far up the fairway as possible, and approach shots where you're hitting into a green. Let's deal with them separately, as they each present a different challenge.

On what I call 'transport' shots from the rough, where you're trying to advance the ball and give yourself an easy shot to the green, a lofted wood is better than a long iron, for two reasons. The rounded clubhead slides through the grass better, which keeps the face square and increases your chances of hitting a straight shot. With a long iron, grass tends to wrap around the hosel of the club at impact

Trouble Spots

↑ ↑ ↑

Take a wood, placing the ball opposite the left heel.

Sweep it away – don't try to help the ball into the air.

which twists the clubface and causes a crooked shot. Secondly, a lofted wood will give you more distance. From rough even an average strike with a wood will be as good as a perfect strike with an iron, because you'll get more run on the ball with a wood shot.

The technique is no different from any other shot with a lofted wood. Put the ball opposite your left heel and try to sweep it away. Don't try to help the ball into the air – you'll top it. You don't need to force it, either. Let the club generate the height and distance you need.

Again, I think a three-quarter swing is the best policy. It helps you make better contact so you can control the ball flight more consistently. If you're thrashing shots out of the rough as hard as you can, there's no way you can make accurate contact or be certain how the ball will fly. It becomes a lottery.

On approach shots from rough, two things can happen. If the grass is very lush the ball tends to come out very soft, so you lose distance. If the rough is dry and wispy you can get a flier, which adds distance.

Read the lie and try to predict how the ball will come out. Then position it two or three inches further back in your stance than normal to promote a steeper angle of attack.

A three-quarter swing should ensure a balanced finish.

For a good approach shot from the rough, try to read the lie.

→ Paul McGinley
Power through deep rough

The key to playing this shot well is to get the ball to come out of the rough with as much control as possible and land softly on the putting surface. To achieve this, you need to get the ball to pitch on the fringe or just on the edge of the green, and run out to the pin. With only a few feet of fringe to work with it is easy to quit on the shot and let the club get tangled in the long rough. But with my method and a lot of practice the shot can become easy.

Do not let your wrists roll over. The clubface needs to stay open through impact, keeping the loft on the club, helping the ball pop out of the rough.

Accelerate steeply into the back of the ball.

Select a 60-degree lob wedge and open up the clubface.

Stance is narrow, feet just a few inches apart.

Pick the club up steeply with plenty of wrist-break, increasing the loft on the club as you do so.

Backswing should be no longer than waist-height.

Ball position is just backward of centre – this will help you make a more descending, clean blow into the back of the ball.

Weight is 70 per cent on the left side, leaning into the shot.

Aim your body, feet and shoulders slightly left of the target line.

Make a full shoulder turn.

Use a running chip shot to beat bumpy terrain

The thing that makes this shot so good is that it's a straightforward solution to a tricky little problem. Having to chip up and over a steep bank between your ball and the flag is a pretty common scenario, especially around raised greens. The worst thing you can do in this predicament is reach for a lofted club, but my guess is that's exactly the option many amateurs would take. Think again. Reach for a mid-iron – on this occasion I'm using a 6-iron – and play the shot low to the ground.

Make sure you set up with your left hand in front of the ball. The idea then is to keep it in front of the ball at impact and feel that you swing the club just like you do for a long putt. Your set-up should encourage the correct strike, with the ball back in your stance and your weight favouring the front foot. But as I said, the key is keeping your left hand in front of the ball at impact and making sure you don't try to help the ball into the air. The ball will skip along the ground with no backspin to check its progress.

Trouble Spots

↑ ↑ ↑

1 I bet you'd normally take a pitching or sand wedge for a shot like this. Try a mid-iron instead, and play the shot close to the ground.

2 Grip low on the club – hands in front of the ball, remember – and swing as you would for a long putt.

3 Keep your hands in front of the ball at impact, and make sure you don't try to help it up into the air.

4 The ball should skip along the ground without backspin. Obstacles like this bank may slow the ball, so adjust for that.

Back-hander

Stymied by a tree? No problem. While you may previously have thought about taking a drop or attempting a left-handed shot when the ball has finished close to an obstacle, this back-handed chip is often the best solution, and is surprisingly easy to play.

It has to be a lofted club

This shot is only possible with a lofted club, since a more straight-faced iron sits too much on the toe. Experiment to see which suits you best, but probably a pitching wedge is the one to choose.

Simple technique

Ball position is important – just in front of your feet – so you can strike the ball with a descending blow. Stand with your back square to the target line.

No wrist-break

The idea is, if you keep your wrist firm the less can go wrong with the swing. It is purely a pendulum action – straight up and down, dropping the blade crisply on to the back of the ball. Wrist-break should only occur on the follow-through if needed.

➡️ **Bradley Dredge**
Get distance out of a divot

It's every golfer's biggest nightmare. You hit a great drive down the middle of the fairway, only to find your ball embedded in a nasty divot – and you're still 200 yards from the green. But don't panic, this misfortune needn't be a card-killer. There are two simple ways to play this shot: the low, running long iron or the high, cutting fairway wood. Club selection will depend on the trouble ahead. If you can run the ball up to the green, select a long iron; if you have to carry a hazard, such as water, then a fairway wood is the better option. The long iron will be played with a low hook so that it only flies about two-thirds of its usual length and then runs the rest of the way up to the hole. The fairway wood is played as a high cut shot so that it flies high and lands softly, carrying the trouble and landing majestically on to the putting surface.

Use a long iron or fairway wood when faced with a long shot from a divot.

↑ ↑ ↑ ↑

Low, hooking long iron

Grip down the club as the ball is quarter-of-an-inch lower than normal.

High, cutting fairway wood

Grip down the club slightly.

Aim

Aim your body slightly right of the target to allow for a draw. Aim the clubface square to the target.

Ball position

Well back. Between the middle and your back foot.

Aim

Aim the body 10-15 yards left of the target. The worse the lie, the further left you should aim. Aim the club straight at the target.

Ball position

An inch or two back in the stance from normal set-up.

➡️ Robert Allenby
Don't let a tree trouble you

Anyone who tells you a tree is 90 per cent air is talking rubbish. If you try to hit straight through it you're bound to catch the branches; that's why you need to know how to shape the ball around the tree. It's one of the easiest shots to learn. All you have to do is bring the ball back a couple of inches in your stance, aim the clubface at the target, then turn your body about 45 degrees so that you are aiming at a point maybe as much as 30 yards right of the target. From there all you have to do is make a normal swing. Because the club is shut in relation to your body alignment, the ball will start out to the right and hook back, right around the tree and on to the green. Easy!

Body aims right
Your feet, knees, hips and shoulders aim right of the target, as far as 30 yards.

Stance
Take your normal stance, feet a shoulder-width apart.

Clubface
Should aim at the target (this will be shut in relation to your body alignment).

Ball position
Move the ball forwards a couple of inches from the middle to the front of your stance, just inside your left toe.

The hanging lie – three ways to play the downhill chip

The first way

The steeper the incline of the slope, the harder the shot, therefore the more loft on the club you'll need. Choose your most lofted club and play a very high shot. Aim to land the ball just on the front of the green; where it will release.

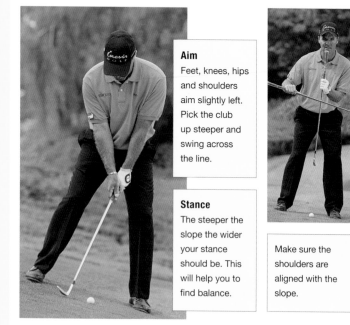

Aim
Feet, knees, hips and shoulders aim slightly left. Pick the club up steeper and swing across the line.

Stance
The steeper the slope the wider your stance should be. This will help you to find balance.

Make sure the shoulders are aligned with the slope.

Hands
Keep the hands central. Don't push them ahead; this will shut the club-face, giving a low flight.

Weight distribution
Lean with the slope and keep the majority of weight on the lower foot for balance.

Trouble Spots

⬆ ⬆ ⬆

1 Use a wristy action to pick the club up steeply, ensuring it doesn't hit the bank.

2 Do not try to help the ball off the slope. Play the ball down the slope, allowing the loft on the club to get the ball in the air.

3 Vary the length of your follow-through depending on how far you have to hit the ball. The longer your follow-through the further the ball will travel.

Common mistakes

The biggest problem with the downhill shot is getting yourself set up to the ball comfortably so that you don't lose balance. To do this you must set yourself up to lean with the slope. If your weight is wrong it will lead to poor shots.

Leaning back causes the club to return high up the ball …

… causing you to swing up and out and thin the shot.

Leaning too much into the slope will cause a fat shot.

The second way

If you are scared of using the high method (sand wedge) then this is a very useful alternative to practise. Instead of flying the ball on to the fringe, choose a less lofted club such as an 8- or 7-iron and run the ball down the slope.

The technique

You only need a very short backswing and follow-through as you want the ball to pitch only a few feet in front of you and then run down the slope.

Set-up

Grip down the club and set up so that you lean with the slope for balance again.

Ball position

Play the ball slightly back in your stance to avoid the club bouncing off the turf into the ball.

Remember

This is a more risky shot as it is hard to predict the bounce you will get and the weight you need to hit it to run down the slope.

On a steeper slope put the ball further back in your stance.

The third way

If you are lucky to have only a slight downhill slope to contend with then the easiest option will be to use a putter. This takes away the unpredictability of the bounce. If the grass on the slope is very smooth then there is no benefit in lifting the ball above it; putting the ball is the safest option.

The technique
Use your normal putting stroke to putt the ball down the slope. Keep the putter low to the ground, back and through, concentrating on making a solid connection.

Posture
Stand so that your body is perpendicular to the slope, leaning in the same direction.

Hand position
Position your hands the same as for your normal putting stroke, slightly in front of the ball.

Ball position
Slightly back in the stance, about centre, to prevent you hitting the slope before the ball.

Up against the cut

I often find myself playing on courses where the green, fringe, fairway and rough are really well defined. While the courses look great like this, it can make shot-making very difficult, particularly if my ball finishes up against two cuts of different length grass. For instance, when the ball is right up against the fringe of the green it can be difficult to play either a chip or a putt. The easiest solution is to play

Ball position
This should be off the back foot to help keep the hands ahead of the ball.

Grip
Use your normal putting grip. And grip softly.

Stance
Narrow your stance with your feet almost together.

⬆ ⬆ ⬆

what I call the 'bladed shot'. Take a lofted club, such as your pitching wedge, and grip it like a putter, but make sure you grip right down the end to give you more control. The ball should be positioned off your back foot. Now hover the blade edge of the wedge halfway up the ball; aiming to strike it on its equator, and swing back and through, rocking the shoulders to make your putting stroke. You don't need to swing too hard, as this will put a lot of topspin on the ball. Instead of 'hitting' at it, you only need to get it just about rolling like a putt. This eliminates the danger of a duffed putt.

Follow-through
Aim to strike the ball on its equator, then hit through the ball. Don't 'hit' at it.

→ → → Putting

F ew things are more frustrating than hitting the green in regulation only to take three or four putts. Yet among amateurs it's an all too common scenario, turning a potentially good round into a disastrous one. Putting may looks deceptively simple, but as any pro who has suffered from the dreaded yips will tell you, it's as challenging a part of the game as any other, if not more. As well as the problem of getting the technique right, there's the complication of reading the line and judging the speed, both of which, if you get them wrong, can make you look rather foolish. So then, if there's any one shot worth focusing on, it's surely this. Read on, and learn to putt like a champion.

⊕ Ken Brown

Use a pre-shot routine

Throughout my career as a player I adopted a consistent set-up routine. Henry Cotton put me on to this when I went to see him in Portugal. He said that once you've lined up a putt, you should do the same thing every time up to the point where you strike the ball. He was right, of course.

A good set-up procedure gets you focused. It stands up to pressure because it helps you treat every putt the same. It's absolutely fundamental to putting well. So give my method a try.

Line up the putt from the same distance behind the ball, and from the same height. I used to crouch down six feet behind the ball (just as the wonderful putter Bobby Locke used to do) because getting the same perspective every time made me more adept at identifying breaks. If you stand in a different spot to read each putt you get a different perspective, which is confusing on the eye. Having lined up the putt, I then get up slowly, no rush, and walk up to the ball, all the time keeping my eye on the line of the putt and visualizing the ball rolling along it. I adopt my stance, line up the putter to the side of the ball and take two practice putting strokes. Finally, I address the ball, take one final look at the hole, and strike the putt.

Line up the putt from the same distance behind the ball every time.

Keep your eye on the line of the putt as you approach the ball.

Putting

↑ ↑ ↑

144

Reading the putt

Correct alignment is the most important part of putting, because no matter how good your stroke is, if you don't read the line correctly and aim at the right place, then it is going to miss. You have to pick your line and trust it.

Don't change your mind. Commit to the stroke. Being decisive and wrong is better than being indecisive.

Get down low and look at the hole from both sides. This will show you the break of slope on the ground.

Aim at the point where the ball will start to break in towards the hole. Imagine a line tracing from the hole back through this point to your ball.

Seve Ballesteros

Soft hands keep the putter on track

When putting, exert the same pressure with both hands. If you are holding the putter tight with one hand and not the other, the putter will tend to drift off line. Grip lightly with both hands – even a small child should be able to pull the putter from you without much effort.

Seve holds the putter lightly, exacting the same gentle pressure with both hands.

Putting

↑ ↑ ↑

Nick Dougherty
Putt hands-free

The most common mistake I see amateurs making is to involve their hands in the putting action. The hinge movement in the hands breaks the strike and will lead to an inconsistent stroke. One way to counter this is to grip the club lightly. This will encourage a relaxed, fluid putt, rather than a jerky, tense stroke. This simple drill will help you take the hands out of the action, helping to keep the putter far more steady and on line.

1 Grip the putter in the fingers like there's a bird in your hands. The lighter you grip the better feel and response you will get from the putter.

2 Feel that your two hands are pulling away from each other, to remove any wrist movement.

3 Your shoulders and arms should form a triangle. Simply rock the shoulders, keeping the arms working together as one unit.

Develop a rock-solid putting stroke

The whole essence of successful putting lies in creating a stroke that delivers the putter to the back of the ball on the correct line, with the face square, travelling at the right speed. Sounds easy, but of course it's not, although Annika Sörenstam sometimes makes it look so. She's a beautiful putter, which is partly why she's the most dominant female golfer in the world right now. Annika's method is a popular one in the pro game; one which can easily help others in the amateur game. It basically is a shoulder-controlled movement. The shoulders rock, while the hands and wrists stay quite passive, and the putter swings back and forth. If the ball is opposite the left heel, as it should be, then the putter meets it on a gentle upward arc. This sweeps the ball away and creates a nice roll. Easy!

Like all really fine putters, there's no hit as such in Annika's stroke. It's more of a smoothly accelerating swing.

Putting

↑ ↑ ↑

Keep your hands and wrists fairly passive and just let the putter respond to the rocking of the shoulders.

Your putter will impart topspin if the ball is positioned forward in your stance at address. This will make it roll better.

Keep your head still through impact. Only look up when the ball is well on its way to the hole.

The shoulder action is a rocking motion – left shoulder down in the backswing, right shoulder down in the throughswing.

⊙ Michael Campbell
'Walk your eyes' up the line

Michael Campbell's coach points out that many golfers' routines do not prepare them for the stroke: 'I see a lot of golfers go through what I would call a ritual which really doesn't prepare them to make a proper putt. You need to attach more emotion to what you're doing. A good routine is like a comfort bubble, it protects you from pressure. Michael works hard on "walking his eyes" up and down the line at the same speed as a real putt. I have timed his laser-like stare and it is identical to the time it takes for the ball to roll into the cup moments later.'

'Walking the eyes'
2.8 seconds

Real putt
2.8 seconds

Speed is everything

I get asked all the time about how to become a better putter. My reply is always the same. If you learn nothing else about putting, remember this – speed is everything, line is secondary. When I practise, all I work on is how I'm going to control the speed of the ball.

I always get a kick out of watching amateurs in pro-ams. From distances of 30 or 40 feet they'll say: 'It's two balls outside the right edge.' Forget it!

Just aim to the left or right of the hole and concentrate on rolling the ball at the right speed around the cup. If you have the wrong speed on a putt, there's no sense even thinking about line anyway.

As for the stroke itself, you need something that's repeatable and which you feel allows you to control the speed of the ball. I recommend controlling the speed of putts using the length of your backstroke. You need to develop this so that it totally determines how far the ball's going to roll. The actual tempo of your stroke should remain consistent.

The other thing you must work on is striking the ball solidly. You can't afford to have a stroke that doesn't connect solidly out of the middle of the putter-face; otherwise the ball comes off the face at different speeds.

The technique

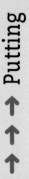

Loren's putting stroke is wonderfully simple. He stands tall and swings the putter with a shoulders-and-arms movement. His hands stay relatively passive, the tempo is smooth and unhurried, and the strike is pure.

Putting

↑ ↑ ↑

Get the ball rolling

I've changed my putting style several times, but I've had one constant aim
– to give the ball a good roll. A good roll means the ball hugs the ground
from the moment it leaves the putter. This is vital, because if the ball gets
airborne – either through being hit into the ground and popping up, or
being hit upward – it bounces, and that makes it impossible to control
speed or line. You will never hole putts, especially those with break, if the
ball is bouncing around. One way of ensuring a consistent strike is to have
the same length of backswing and follow-through.

A good roll on a putt means the ball
hugs the ground from the moment
it leaves the putter-face.

How to read a long putt

There's no real science to reading putts. It's more of an art and, like most things in that field, some are better at it than others. Tiger's pretty good – no shock there. But teaching yourself to become a better reader of putts is a matter of experience, habit and trust. Adhere to a few golden rules, have the discipline to do the same thing on every putt, and when you're over the ball stick to your original conclusion. If you fulfil that part of the bargain, your pay-off will be better long putts, finishing close to or in the hole.

Good read
When you crouch down to read a putt, make sure you stay the same distance from the ball every time, so your eyes get accustomed to that perspective.

Putting

↑ ↑ ↑

Walk along the entire length of a putt and have a good look at the last few feet leading up to the hole. Often you'll spot subtle breaks that you might not have seen from behind the ball.

Trust yourself and stick to the line. So many amateurs get over the putt and start doubting themselves; nearly always that results in an under-read and the ball slips by on the low side.

Even if the ball doesn't look like it's going in, keep your eyes on it, especially if it runs past the hole. You can get a good clue as to how the return putt will break.

Keep your head still

Keeping your head down is one of the worst tips that exists for the full swing, but for anyone wanting to hole more putts it's sound advice. And there are many ways you can do it. Over short putts you can wait for the sound of the ball dropping into the hole (hopefully!) before you look up. That works.

A more popular method, which a lot of tour pros swear by, is marking and replacing the ball in such a way that the logo is exactly where you intend to strike the ball. This gives you something specific to keep your eye on. And without a doubt keeping your eye on the ball is an absolute fundamental to pure striking – you need to see the ball being hit. If you move your head too early you'll never hit the same spot on the putter-face twice. It's like driving a car; if you move your eyes to the left your car veers that way. Same in putting. If you let your eyes wander the putter goes with them.

Even better, draw your own identification mark on the ball. I think I was the first golfer on tour to do this. Now I doubt there's a single golfer who doesn't. There are lots of variations you can use – a line along the logo is popular because as well as giving you something to focus on, it helps you line up in the direction you want the ball to start.

Mark and replace your ball so that the logo is positioned where you intend to strike it.

Putting

⬆ ⬆ ⬆

Padraig Harrington

Putt cross-handed

I decided to switch hands and putt with my left hand below my right at Tour Qualifying School. I comfortably secured my card and I've never looked back, nor has my putting stroke. With a conventional grip the left shoulder is distinctly higher than the right, which doesn't help when you're trying to produce the perfect pendulum putting stroke. The cross-handed grip helps get your shoulders level at address, which promotes an on-line stroke. If you have already got confidence in your putting and hole loads of putts there's no reason to change, but if you're struggling it's worth a try.

Alignment
Putting with your left hand below the right squares the shoulders.

⊙ **Paul McGinley**
Positive putting

Positive thinking is the key to sinking putts whether it be in a match-play or strokeplay situation. When I was stood over the final putt on the 18th green at The Belfry in 2002, I knew how important it was and that it was for the Ryder Cup. Yet the only thing that was going through my mind was to get the correct line. I knew that if I got the line right, all I had to do was have the nerve to commit to the putt, put a good stroke on the ball, and it would go in. Fortunately it did! To have the opportunity to hole that putt was magnificent, and to actually hole it was a dream come true. Putting shouldn't be a nerve-racking aspect of the game, but a positive one. And the more you practise, the less worried about your putts you will be.

Ball position should be slightly forward of centre. This will encourage a better strike, as hitting the ball on the up-stroke puts a good roll on the ball.

Putting

↑ ↑ ↑

Great putters have one thing in common – they are all positive. They don't just let their putts trickle into the back of the hole – they hit them in with a positive, confident stroke. The old saying, 'never up, never in' is one of the most appropriate in golf, because if you leave the putt short it will never go in! So always putt positively and give the ball a chance of dropping into the hole.

Don't look at the hole, but at a spot one to two inches beyond the cup.

Make a positive stroke and the ball should hit the back of the hole as it drops.

➔ Niclas Fasth
Judge your speed

People usually struggle because they don't practise. That is the harsh reality. The good thing is, putting is an easy part of the game to improve on and a little can go a long way. The secret is judgment of speed. Speed is everything – it determines how you read a putt and how you hit a putt.

When you look at a putt, the first thing to decide is how hard you want to hit it as this determines the line. The firmer you hit it, the less the ball will break. From that, you can create a picture in your mind of the ball's path towards the hole. And that is very important. It means you're thinking positively and have a goal. A lot of people hit putts with no real goal; they just send the ball somewhere towards the hole.

Then, as you prepare to putt, keep that mental picture in your mind. Always have at least one practice swing, and as you do, think 'how big a swing do I need in order to roll the ball smoothly to the hole?' That's your only thought. Nothing technical. Try to feel in your stroke how hard you're going to hit it. Then stand over the ball, and hit it, without thinking too much about anything else. It's all about feel.

Putting

↑ ↑ ↑

1 On any putt, let speed determine how you visualize the line, not vice versa.

2 Keep that image uppermost in your mind as you make practice strokes.

3 Once you're over the ball, don't delay ...

4 ... simply strike the putt as you imagined it.

Action point

Keep your routine the same every time by consciously repeating it until it becomes almost second nature. A routine is vital. It gives your mind-set some consistency; a kind of security, if you like. And crucially, it helps you think about what you're trying to do (hole the putt), rather than what you don't want to happen (miss it!).

Ensure your palms face each other

I've always believed that no matter what technique you use, the palms of your hands should be facing one another at address, and square to the target line. I know there are certain exceptions to this rule, such as the grip of Chris di Marco, but that doesn't make it any less relevant. You'll find a lot of top players would agree.

If you have the palms facing at address, they naturally want to return to a square position as they swing into impact. That means there's no manipulation required in order to return the putter squarely to the back of the ball. It's like when you clap your hands. The palms naturally return to face one another; you don't have to think about it.

If the palms aren't facing at address, they tend to work independently, so one hand becomes more dominant than the other. That's not good news, because it tends to throw the putter off its natural swinging arc.

If you have the palms facing at address, they naturally want to return to a square position.

Before you grip the club, position the hands as if you're about to clap.

Grip the club and ensure the palms of your hands are still facing. Perfect.

Putting

↑ ↑ ↑

➡ Stewart Cink

Belly putting

I changed to a belly putter a few years ago and it has made a massive difference to my putting stats – in 2002 I was 112th in the US but two years later I was ranked No. 1. I used to be a very wristy putter. My left wrist would come up and out of the putt, causing me to slice across the ball and miss a lot of putts right of the hole. The belly putter takes the wrists out of the putting action and stops you manipulating the putter-head. This allows you to concentrate on the sensation of rocking the arms and shoulders as one unit and teaches you to stay very still over the ball with no unnecessary body movement. I found it really easy to make the switch and with a bit of practice you could, too.

Let your hands release freely through the putt.

Rock your arms and shoulders back and through.

The belly putter is particularly effective from short range where you don't want any wrist movement at all.

Remember
When you are choosing a belly putter it is really important that you get one that is cut to the right length for you. It should rest in the pit of your stomach (your sternum) so that you feel totally comfortable when you address the ball.

⊕ Nick Dougherty

Get a good ball roll

This is especially important in the winter when you are playing on uneven putting surfaces. If you can put a good roll on the ball then you are giving it a much greater chance of going in.

The hands should be in line with the ball. Do not push them forward as this de-lofts the putter.

Adopt a forward ball position so that you hit on the up, causing less backspin.

Putting

↑ ↑ ↑ ↑

Keep the putter-head low to the ground on the way back and through.

Mark the line

It is great to hit towering drives off the tee but the majority of players would reduce their scores significantly if they holed out a bit better over a round of golf. Here is a very simple tip that you can use while playing, which should make you hole more putts.

Line your ball
Put a straight line on your ball with a marker pen. I use an arrow to give me the image of the ball rolling into the hole.

Aim the putter
Having read the break of the putt, simply line the arrow with where you want the ball to begin. And then aim your putter-face perpendicular to the line on the ball.

Putting

↑ ↑ ↑

Why it works

1 It will make you commit to picking an exact line on every putt, so it will enhance your green-reading skills.

2 It will let you see immediately if you have mishit the putt, as the arrow will not roll end-over-end like it does on a good strike.

3 It will make you much more aware of the pace at which you hit the ball.

You will soon become very aware that the perfect read doesn't ensure a good putt. If you hit it too soft, the ball breaks too much and you miss it on the low side; too hard and the ball goes through the break and you miss it on the high side of the hole.

4 It will give you something to focus your attention on when you get under pressure. Rather than worrying about the putt or what the putt could mean, you can focus purely on rolling the ball along the line.

Golf Tips from the Pros 165

→ → → Practice

A significant part of playing golf well is talent or natural ability, call it what you will, but it's not the main part. Even the greatest golfers make time for regular practice, working hard on every aspect of their game. Indeed, many would say that the secret of their success lies in just that: innumerable hours of dedicated effort on the practice ground. Amateurs, of course, have less time at their disposal for this than professionals and, quite understandably, most prefer the buzz of a game to the chore of practice, but if you want to see your game improve it's the latter that will help you succeed. And, as the following tips show, even a little practice can make a huge difference to the way you play and the scores you shoot.

Fail to prepare ... prepare to fail

Preparation for play is the bread and butter of my profession; it is the key to ensuring I play each course to the best of my ability and make a good living. For amateurs who play the game for recreation it is obviously going to be much less of a priority. Convincing someone to go and spend an afternoon at the driving range or getting to know a course they've never played is much harder than offering them a leisurely game of golf, though I hope that showing you how I prepare before a tournament will help you to improve your own practice time.

Practice drills
Groove your stroke by using two or three balls from every position.

Constructive practice

1 It goes without saying that practice is an important part of any proper preparation for a tournament. But the main difference between professionals and amateurs is the way they use practice time. Professionals are extremely thorough and spend hours every day practising many different shots to ensure that no part of their game is neglected. For most amateurs, who work during the week and just play at weekends, this is unrealistic, but even the odd hour in the evening will help you make improvements. I suggest that you use your practice time to work on the weakest parts of your game.

For most players that's the short game. The great thing is that you can practise many of these shots at home, like chipping in the garden or putting on the carpet.

The most important thing is to feel good about every aspect of your game before a competition. If you're worried about your putting it will let you down, so practise it!

Know what to work on

2 I like the saying 'practice doesn't make perfect, it makes permanent'. It's a great way of illustrating that unless you are practising the right things you won't improve.

Taking regular lessons with a professional is really important as your pro can make sure you don't slip into any bad habits.

The best way to prepare for a competition is to have a few simple drills or swing thoughts to work on at the range. I'm not a mechanical player so I try to keep things simple and just concentrate on my body turn, making sure I don't overswing. All players can do this to help with timing, which is key to ball-striking consistency.

On-course situation simulation

3 It's not often you'll get the opportunity to play a course before a competition, but when you do it's really important to make the most of that practice round. Play from as many different positions on the course as possible – from the fairway, the rough, the bunkers, you name it – and play several balls on every hole. Limiting yourself to playing one ball inevitably means you won't feel as familiar with all aspects of the course as you should. Practising from different positions will leave you feeling much more prepared and will take away the element of surprise if your ball finishes in an awkward position during the competition.

Synchronize
I concentrate on the timing of my body turn, making sure I don't overswing. This keeps my swing controllable.

I practise from the rough and the fairway. You should too.

Adaptability
Try to adapt your shot-making skills to suit the course you're playing. I concentrate on practising shots that are most applicable to the course conditions, particularly greenside, like bump-and-runs for firm links turf or lofted wedge shots out of dense Bermuda grass.

The Woods warm-up

The more time you can spend warming up those key muscles the better you can expect to play, and the greater the chance of nailing that first drive of the day. If you haven't got the time or inclination to follow the Tiger Woods warm-up routine, don't worry. Even if you've only got 10 minutes before your tee-off you can still do a few stretches to get your muscles ready for action. Try this quick drill. Place a club across your shoulders and rotate back and through as if you're making a golf swing. Repeat five or six times. Rest assured this is better than just stepping up to your first drive and hoping it will fly long and straight. More often than not it won't.

Practice ↑ ↑ ↑

Tiger Woods will start his warm-up by spending the first five minutes hitting a sand wedge. He'll hit several shots different distances from a range of 25 yards to 100.

He'll then move up to an 8-iron before switching to a 5-iron. With both clubs he'll hit a series of straight shots before executing draws and fades.

Fairway woods off the deck will be followed by his driver off the tee. Then to wind up his 30-minute session on he range, Tiger will hit a couple of shots with his 8-iron and finally the sand wedge.

The final half-hour before tee-off will be spent chipping, playing bunker shots and finally putting. Then it's off to the first tee to compose himself. More often than not he'll then nail his first drive.

Make the most of practice

Try to set aside at least one day a week to practise, and plan your day out the night before.

Next time you go to the range leave enough time to hit each club in your bag 10 times. Measure how far the ball goes and take the average for each club. I use a laser range-finder to measure the distances. Then write these down on a piece of paper and put it in your bag. When you're on the course make sure you know how far you have to the flag on every shot and refer to your yardage chart to select the right club. Remember – the distance you hit your clubs can change depending on the conditions you're playing in. Generally, if it's raining, take an extra club, and if it's warm and dry, perhaps one less.

If you don't have a lot of time to practise then the best way to improve is to concentrate on the parts of your game that can save you the most shots. For most players, this is usually the short game. The most important club in your bag is the putter, followed by wedges, short irons and, lastly, the driver.

Keep it varied
Never practise any one thing for more than 30 minutes because your attention will wander and you'll put too much stress on that part of the body.

Practice

↑ ↑ ↑

⏩ Ian Poulter

Always place clubs on the ground

It's very rare that I hit practice balls without a club on the ground to help me with my alignment. It's especially important on those first dozen or so shots in a session, when you're feeling your way a bit and trying to get your swing into the groove. That's the time when you really don't want to be training bad habits.

Imagine a train track leading to the target. The ball should be on the right rail and your toes along the left rail. Lay a club down to get your alignment right.

Remember this

Developing a repeatable, consistent golf swing is often about doing the simple things well. Alignment is a classic example. By placing clubs on the ground you're constantly reinforcing good habits; basically, training yourself to instinctively do the right thing on the golf course. Don't waste the opportunity.

Transfer your weight in the backswing

A common fault with amateurs is poor weight transfer in the back-swing. They get a little 'stuck' on the front foot as they swing the club back and fall backwards as they swing the club down. It's the reverse of what should happen, hence the term 'reverse pivot'. Here's a practice drill I work on sometimes.

Tee a ball up and address it using a 7-iron. Draw your left foot back so the toe is level with your right heel. Now make the best backswing turn you can, feeling that your weight loads on to your right side. If you have just one thought, try to get your left shoulder directly over your flexed right knee. From there, transfer your weight on to your front foot as you swing smoothly down and through, clipping the ball off the tee peg.

Within the space of a few minutes you should start to feel the benefits of making a better weight transfer. And in half an hour, you'll be hitting sweet little draw shots.

Tee a ball up and address it using a 7-iron. Draw your left foot back.

Practice

↑ ↑ ↑

Other benefits come as part of the deal. You should feel that the knees are braced and offering support as you swing back and through. Also, having your left foot drawn back gives you an enhanced feeling of clearing the left side out of the way in the hitting area, so you can release the club freely down the target line.

Make the best backswing turn you can, feeling your weight loading on to your right side.

Transfer your weight on to your front foot as you swing smoothly down and through.

Make the transition from drill to proper swing

As with any practice drill the real measure of success is being able to integrate the same feelings into your proper swing. This is best achieved by hitting alternate shots – one drill, one normal – at the range. With repetition, you'll get there in the end.

Make a smooth takeaway

This is a practice drill I use quite a lot to ensure I get a good take-away. One of the main problems I used to suffer from was that my initial takeaway movement involved a lot of upper body action. The consequence of my early body movement was that I would lose my balance easily. And that would cause me a lot of problems through the shot.

With a more controlled takeaway it is much easier to keep your balance throughout the swing. To prevent upper body movement and to focus my attention on the club moving away I use this drill to get the right feel at the very start of my swing.

Practice

↑ ↑ ↑

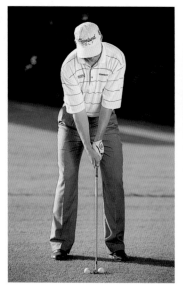

Place a ball directly behind your club at address but make sure it is on the ball-to-target line.

Focus on letting the club follow the ball-to-target line on your takeaway.

I place a ball directly behind my clubhead along the ball-to-target line, and then focus on getting the club to roll the ball backwards as I begin my take-away. This promotes a good, smooth, one-piece action rather than a jerky movement. The trick is to get the ball rolling gradually.

Roll the ball
Make sure you roll the ball out of the way with the back of the clubhead.

Drill to cure your slice

The most common weak shot amateurs suffer from is the slice. This is purely the result of not training your hands to roll and release the club. I was taught this drill from an early age to help me get the feel of putting a right-to-left draw on the ball and I still use it when I'm warming up at the practice ground to get that feeling in the hands.

First, set up to the ball as you would for a normal shot. Now simply step forward a foot with your left foot. This will give you a closed body position in relation to the target.

Swing path
The club gets forced on an 'in-to-out' swing path to the right of your target.

Practice

↑ ↑ ↑ ↑

A closed body position is forced due to the left foot being forward.

Your downswing will be an in-to-out path and should result in a draw.

Now swing back like normal; you will find that on your downswing your upper body is forced to swing out to the right.

From this position, all you have to do is make sure you roll your wrists over and release the club and you should put a fantastic sweeping draw on the ball. It may feel a bit odd at first.

Feet
Left foot in front of right.

Wrist roll
Concentrate on the roll of the wrists, releasing the club.

 Thomas Levet
Chip to a piece of paper

Many amateurs struggle to judge the weight of their chip shots around the green because they simply don't know how hard to hit the shot. Rather than getting up and down they end up taking three or four shots from the edge of the green. To keep things simple, I always aim to land the ball at a point one metre on the green.

When I practise I mark this spot with chalk, or tee a piece of paper into the ground. Then to get a feel of how hard I need to hit the shot I simply throw the ball on to the paper and let it run out. When you chip the shot you need to use this feeling to judge the length of your swing.

Then, to change the distance the ball goes you simply need to change clubs. For a close pin choose a sand wedge; pitch on to the paper, and the ball will only run out a short distance. For a pin that's further away, select a less-lofted club such as a 7-iron.

Get hands-on
Prepare for your chipping session by throwing the ball to the piece of paper. This will help you learn to judge the length of swing required.

Practice
↑ ↑ ↑ ↑

In the swing

With a selection of clubs and using the same length swing, chip to a piece of paper teed into the ground. This will improve your judgment of carry and roll.

➔ Ian Poulter
Chip to your umbrella

Stick an upturned brolly in the ground and scatter balls around, at distances ranging from 10 yards right up to 50 yards, if space permits. Then work your way from one ball to the next, lobbing balls full pitch into the brolly.

Take your time with each shot. Visualize what you're trying to do and make practice swings to get a feel for the length and pace of the swing required. It's the fast-track way to teach yourself the art of pitching the ball on a chosen spot from a variety of distances. It's about feel.

Practising from different distances should give you that elusive 'feel' around the green.

Practice ↑ ↑ ↑ ↑

Remember this
If your short game is a bit scrappy pick one club, a wedge of some description, and stick with that. Make it your favourite. Get your confidence levels up before you start playing around with different clubs to pitch and chip.

Paul Casey
Practise reading greens

It's something no one really does but everyone should do. If you think about it, reading greens is an art that you can only learn through hard work and practise, and that is just as important as the stroke itself. And yet people don't spend nearly as long practising it as they do their putting stroke. You can have a perfect putting stroke and hit the perfect shot; but if you can't work out the direction the ball is meant to go in, then it's not going to go in the hole. Learn to visualize the line.

With a friend, find a sidehill putt and put a tee in the ground where you think you have to start the ball for it to go in the hole. Then get your friend to have a look at the line and do the same. Hit putts along both lines and see who was right. Most amateurs consistently under-read the amount of break in a putt and miss on the low side. This drill will help to train your reading of greens.

Amateurs who I play with tend, as a rule, not to allow for enough break and will usually aim at the white tee. The yellow tee is the correct line to aim for, the break taking the ball into the hole.

Putting around the clock

Putting is the most important aspect of the game but it's often the most boring thing to practise. That's why I jazz up my practice sessions by using a couple of simple drills I've picked up from other players on Tour. I like Phil Mickelson's 'around the clock' drill as it teaches you both pace and alignment. Simply pop four tee pegs down in a clockwise direction, measuring one putter-length distance from the hole. Start at tee peg number one and work your way around, holing each putt. Try to set the drill up on a relatively flat part of the green to begin with, in order to train your stroke. As you get more competent move to a slopey green and practice uphill, downhill and across-slope putts, so as to work on your green reading and alignment. Set yourself targets, such as how many putts to hole in a row, and up your goals as you get better.

Measure
Set four tee pegs around the hole about one putter-length distance out.

Set the drill up
on a flat part
of the green to
begin with and
move to a more
slopey area
as you gain
confidence.

Players Profiles

Robert Allenby

Australian; US and Australasian Tour player; turned pro 1991; Presidents Cup team member

Peter Baker

English; Challenge and European Tour player; Ryder Cup team member

Severiano Ballesteros

Spanish; European Tour player; turned pro 1974; Open Champion 1979, 1984 and 1988; US Masters Champion 1980 and 1983; Ryder Cup team member and captain

Ken Brown

English; European Tour player; turned pro 1975; Ryder Cup team member; TV commentator

Michael Campbell

New Zealander; European and Australasian Tour player; turned pro 1993; US Open Champion 2005; President's Cup team member

Paul Casey

English; European and US Tour player; turned pro 2000; Ryder Cup team member

Stewart Cink

American; US Tour player; turned pro 1995; Ryder and Presidents Cup team member

Laura Davies

English, LPGA and Ladies European Tour player; turned pro 1985; US Women's Open Champion 1987; LPGA Champion 1994 and 1996; du Maurier Classic Champion 1996; Solheim Cup team member

Jamie Donaldson

Welsh; European Tour player; turned pro 2000

Nick Dougherty

English; European Tour player; turned pro 2001

Bradley Dredge

Welsh; European Tour player; turned pro 1996

Scott Drummond

Scottish; European Tour player; turned pro 1996

Paul Eales

English; European Tour player; turned pro 1985

Ernie Els

South African; European, US and 'Sunshine' Tour player; turned pro 1989; US Open Champion 1994 and 1997; Open Champion 2002; Presidents Cup team member

Gary Evans

English; European Tour player; turned pro 1991

Nick Faldo

English; European and US Tour player; turned pro 1976; Open Champion 1987, 1990 and 1992; US Masters Champion 1989, 1990 and 1996; Ryder Cup team member

Niclas Fasth

Swedish; European and US Tour player; turned pro 1993

Alastair Forsyth

Scottish; European Tour player; turned pro 1998

Pierre Fulke

Swedish; European Tour player; turned pro 1989; Ryder Cup team member

Fred Funk

American; US Tour player; turned pro 1981; Ryder and Presidents Cup team member

Jim Furyk

American; US Tour player; turned pro 1992; US Open Champion 2003; Ryder and Presidents Cup team member

Retief Goosen

South African; US, European and 'Sunshine' Tour player; turned pro 1990; US Open Champion 2001 and 2004; Presidents Cup team member

Bernard Gallacher

Scottish; European and European Seniors Tour player; turned pro 1967; Ryder Cup team member and Captain

Ian Garbutt

English; European and Challenge Tour player; turned pro 1992

Jay Haas

American; US Tour player; turned pro 1976; Ryder and Presidents Cup team member

Joakim Haeggman

Swedish; European Tour player; turned pro 1989; Ryder Cup team member

Chris Hanell

English; European and Challenge Tour player; turned pro 1992

Padraig Harrington

Irish; European and US Tour player; turned pro 1995; Ryder Cup team member

David Howell

English; European Tour player; turned pro 1995; Ryder Cup team member

Peter Jacobsen

American; US Tour player; turned pro 1976; Ryder Cup team member

Miguel Angel Jiménez

Spanish; European Tour player; turned pro 1982; Ryder Cup team member

Robert Karlsson

Swedish; European Tour player; turned pro 1989

Bernhard Langer

German; European Tour player; turned pro 1972; US Masters Champion 1985 and 1993; Ryder Cup team member and captain

Paul Lawrie

Scottish; European and US Tour player; turned pro 1986; Open Champion 1999; Ryder Cup team member

Thomas Levet

French; European Tour player; turned pro 1988; Ryder Cup team member

Davis Love III

American; US Tour player; turned pro 1985; US PGA Champion 1997; Ryder and Presidents Cup team member

Paul McGinley

Irish; European Tour player; turned pro 1991; Ryder Cup team member

Greg Norman

Australian; European, US, Australasian and Champions Tour player; turned pro 1976; Open Champion 1986 and 1993; Presidents Cup team member

Corey Pavin

American; US Tour player; turned pro 1982; US Open Champion 1995; Ryder and Presidents Cup team member

Gary Player

South African; US, Southern Africa 'Sunshine' and Australasian Tour player; turned pro 1953; Open Champion 1959, 1968 and 1974; US Masters Champion 1961, 1974 and 1978; US PGA Champion 1962 and 1972; US Open Champion 1965; President's Cup team captain

Ian Poulter

English; European and US Tour player; turned pro 1995; Ryder Cup team member

Phillip Price

Welsh; European Tour player; turned pro 1989

Ronan Rafferty

Irish; European Tour Player; turned pro 1981; Ryder Cup team member

Loren Roberts

American; US and Champions Tour player; turned pro 1975; Ryder Cup team member

Justin Rose

English; US and European Tour player; turned pro 1998

Charl Schwartzel

South African; European and 'Sunshine' Tour player; turned pro 2002

Adam Scott

Australian; European and US Tour player; turned pro 2000; Presidents Cup team member

Vijay Singh

Fijian; US and European Tour player; turned pro 1982; US PGA Champion 1998 and 2004; US Masters Champion 2000; Presidents Cup team member

Annika Sörenstam

Swedish; LPGA Tour player (also one appearance on US PGA Tour); turned pro 1993; US Women's Open Champion 1995 and 1996; Kraft Nabisco Champion 2001, 2002 and 2005; LPGA Champion 2003, 2004 and 2005; Women's British Open Champion 2003; Solheim Cup team member

David Toms

American; US Tour player; turned pro 1989; US PGA Champion 2001; Ryder and Presidents Cup team member

Steve Webster

English; European Tour player; turned pro 1995

Lee Westwood

English; European Tour player; turned pro 1993; Ryder Cup team member

Tiger Woods

American; US Tour player; turned pro 1996; US Masters Champion 1997, 2001, 2002, 2005; US PGA Champion 1999 and 2000; US Open Champion 2000 and 2002; Open Champion 2000 and 2005; Ryder and Presidents Cup team member

Ian Woosnam

Welsh; European Tour player; turned pro 1958; US Masters Champion 1991; Ryder Cup team member

page numbers in bold indicate major references

Index

↑

↑

↑